THE WAY OF SALVATION
AS SEEN THROUGH
THE HEIDELBERG CATECHISM

Cornelius VanKempen

This book uses only The King James Version

ISBN: 978-1-5356-0754-4

Contents

Of God The Son
Lord's Day 11

Lord's Day 12

Lord's Day 13

Lord's Day 14

Lord's Day 15

Of The Holy Supper of Our Lord Jesus Christ
Lord's Day 28

Lord's Day 29

Lord's Day 30

Preface

THE HEIDELBERG CATECHISM IS ONE of the three 'Articles of Unity' adopted by the Reformed churches as to our beliefs. The Catechism is known as the 'Book of Comfort.' It brings forth the preciousness of the Triune God, Father, Son, and Holy Ghost, through the God-Man Jesus Christ. It begins with the question, "What is thy only comfort in life and in death?" This is the question which burdened me to write these short meditations using the catechism as a guide to open the Bible as it answers God's requirement. The Heidelberg Catechism was written at the request of Elector Frederick III to bring harmony to the Protestant teaching and to the establishment of the Reformed Faith. He appointed Zacharias Ursinus and Casper Olevianus to write it to address the errors of the day, bringing out the doctrines necessary to know for this life, but also the life to come.

The Catechism is broken down into three categories of the experiences of God's people, misery, deliverance, and gratitude. When meditating on each question and answer I was brought back to the very first question. We often look to much at our own heart and it's failings, forgetting that there is no comfort to be found there. Jesus Christ is the only hope for ruined, hopeless sinners for salvation. *"Look unto me, and be ye saved, all the ends of the earth: for I am God, and there is none else"* (Isaiah 45:22). The Triune God is a necessity in the working of this great salvation, and does so through Jesus Christ the Savior Redeemer as He is revealed by the Holy Ghost to their hearts. May the readers of these meditations experience the love of God as the Electing Father, the Redeeming Son, and the regenerating Holy Spirit, as the only way of salvation, preserving them and bringing them to be with Him in the place prepared in the Father's house. *"No man hath seen God at any time. If we love one another, God dwelleth in us, and his love is perfected in us. Hereby know we that we dwell in him, and he in us, because he hath given us of his Spirit"* (1 John 4:12-13). May those who do not know this God of love be brought to see that the world's love is empty and really not love at all.

The Author

1.
Christ the Believers Only Comfort

"QUESTION 1: WHAT IS THY only comfort?

ANSWER: THAT I WITH BODY and soul, both in life and death, am not my own, but belong unto my faithful Savior Jesus Christ; who, with his precious blood hath fully satisfied for all my sins, and delivered me from all the power of the devil; and so preserves me that without the will of my heavenly Father, not a hair can fall from my head; yea, that all things must be subservient to my salvation, and therefore, by his Holy Spirit, he also assures me of eternal life, and makes me sincerely willing and ready, henceforth, to live unto him."

The catechism opens with a question. What gives you comfort? Every person born in the world is looking for comfort. In today's world, comfort comes from many physical things, a friend, a good home, family, work, and many more too numerous to mention. While all this gives temporary comfort and may be seen as a blessing, there is no lasting satisfaction in them. Why not? They are all creature comforts which allow us to continue on our way to eternity without coming to grips with who we really are, and what we were created for! The Bible, God's revelation of Himself, tells us. *"What? know ye not that your body is the temple of the Holy Ghost which is in you, which ye have of God, and ye are not your own? For ye are bought with a price: therefore glorify God in your body, and in your spirit, which are God's"* (1 Corinthians 6:19-20). We live as if we are our own, but we are not. The Holy Spirit implants life into our dead hearts making this a reality! We see that all the comforts we have been living for will soon be gone! *"And if Christ be in you, the body is dead because of sin; but the Spirit is life because of righteousness. But if the Spirit of him that raised up Jesus from the dead dwell in you, he that raised up Christ from the dead shall also quicken your mortal bodies by his Spirit that dwelleth in you. Therefore, brethren, we are debtors, not to the flesh, to live after the flesh. For if ye live after the flesh, ye shall die: but if ye through the Spirit do mortify the deeds of the body, ye shall live"* (Romans 8:10-13). This is an agonizing lesson to learn, but as in surgery the surgeon cuts away the diseased flesh to again make us healthy. God the Holy Spirit has given us this question and answer to prepare us for the painful surgery necessary to remove all of our earthly corruptions, and be able find this only comfort that restores us into communion with our Creator. *"And this is the will of him that sent me, that every one which seeth the Son, and believeth on him, may have everlasting life: and I will raise him up at the last day"* (John 6:40).

2.
Lessons Necessary to Live in Comfort

QUESTION 2: "How many things are necessary for thee to know, that thou, enjoying this comfort, mayest live and die happily?

ANSWER: Three; The first, how great my sins and miseries are; the second, how I may be delivered from all my sins and miseries; and third, how I shall express my gratitude to God for such deliverance."

The Physician has His plans all laid out to prepare us for the surgery, to expose the reason why the patient is unable to live and die in comfort without this surgery. He must remove our earthly comforts one by one. This is very painful to our flesh, but even more to our mind. This makes us to see that without understanding of our great sins and miseries there will never be a need for deliverance from them. The work of the Holy Spirit is to make us aware of our great dilemma that we are without God and without hope in the world. We do not understand how this can be done, but also learn we cannot go on as we are. God's Word condemns us. "*I am troubled; I am bowed down greatly; I go mourning all the day long*" (Psalm 38:6). The Physician knows precisely what needs to be done. We have brought all this sin and misery on ourselves with no way of deliverance from our side. This becomes our greatest misery. We may have heard of friends who have been delivered. But could it be for me? God knows how to bring His people to the place where all hope is gone. "*For my loins are filled with a loathsome disease: and there is no soundness in my flesh. I am feeble and sore broken: I have roared by reason of the disquietness of my heart*" Psalm 38:7-8). The Holy Spirit is teaching us how great our sins and miseries are, so that we may be delivered from them. This lesson will be taught by Him, revealing the great Deliverer, and we shall express our gratitude for this deliverance. Let us follow the Surgeon at work. He is one that never fails or forgets one step in the recovery of lost, hell-worthy, sinners. We see that it is the work of the Triune God, Father, Son, and Holy Spirit. All this is for His own glory as He brings His people to glorify Him here in this world, but above all to all eternity. "*Thy people shall be willing in the day of thy power*" (Psalm 110:3a). The glory of our eternal home will make the surgery seem so small as all sin and misery shall be gone and our only comfort becomes a reality.

3.
The Heavenly Surgeon at Work

QUESTION: 3. WHENCE KNOWST THOU thy misery?

ANSWER. OUT OF THE LAW of God.

The Surgeon makes His first cut with the knife; this is a life giving cut, exposing a fatal problem, the infection of sin. The word of God is the knife He uses to discover our depravity, and need of cleansing. A hope for a cure wells up in us and fills our heart with a loathing of self, but at the same time a need for Him. This is a paradox, but God will have a willing people in the day of His power. (See Psalm 110:3). We have broken God's law every moment, and to make matters more desperate, the Surgeon is the One offended. This produces fear and is very painful, causing us to cry out, "Woe is me."

QUESTION: 4. WHAT DOTH THE law of God require of us?

ANSWER. CHRIST TEACHES US THAT briefly, Matt. 22:37-40.

"*Thou shalt love the Lord thy God with all thy heart, and with all thy soul, with all thy mind, and with all thy strength; This is the first and the great commandment; and the second is like unto it, Thou shalt love thy neighbour as thyself. On these two commandments hang all the law and the prophets."*

And he, (Jesus) said unto him, Thou hast answered right: this do, and thou shalt live" (See Luke 10:27-28). The law of love was implanted in our hearts by our Creator, but rejected by us in Paradise by our first parents, Adam and Eve, bringing about the void of comfort in our hearts. This deadly infection found must be removed completely before any healing can begin. The Surgeon understands the problem, but also the remedy; the patient cannot understand either of them. He says, *"What I do thou knowest not now; but thou shalt know hereafter"* (John 13:7b). He is bringing us to an end of all our own abilities to cure ourselves. *"Now we know that what things soever the law saith, it saith to them who are under the law: that every mouth may be stopped, and all the world may become guilty before God"* (Romans 3:19). The Surgeon cuts deeper exposing that not only do we not keep God's law, but our very nature is to hate God and our neighbor.

QUESTION: 5. CANST THOU KEEP all these things perfectly?

ANSWER: IN NO WISE; FOR I am prone by nature to hate God and our neighbor.

The Surgeon has not only exposed to the patient their sickness, but revealed that without a complete radical change there will be no cure. We are born with an incurable spiritual disease which can only be eradicated by the death of our old nature. "*The LORD killeth, and maketh alive: he bringeth down to the grave, and bringeth up*" (1 Samuel 2:6). This surgery is a life-long work of cutting and healing so that we may live in comfort here at times, but forever with Him. Are you being made to hate your sinful nature? Have you met this Divine Surgeon who has promised never to forsake the works of His own hands? (See Psalm 138:8).

4.
The Necessity for Continued Surgery Questioned

QUESTION: 6. DID GOD THEN create man so wicked and perverse?

ANSWER: BY NO MEANS; BUT God created man good and after His own image, in true righteousness and holiness, that he might rightly know God his Creator, heartily love Him, and live with Him in eternal happiness to glorify and praise Him.

This question comes from a heart that is convinced of a need of repair, but not that it is in total disrepair. As this question is answered the knife of the Spirit cuts deeper into the heart and reveals the badness which dwells in our heart. This did not come from our Creator. "*Lo, this only have I found, that God hath made man upright; but they have sought out many inventions*" (Ecclesiastes 7:29). The pain of learning the depth and extent of the disease opens our heart for the next question, "Why am I thus?"

QUESTION: 7. WHENCE THEN PROCEEDS this depravity of human nature?

ANSWER: FROM THE FALL AND disobedience of our first parents, Adam and Eve, in Paradise; hence our nature is become so corrupt, that we are all conceived and born in sin.

This rebellion is self inflicted for which the sentence is death. (Read Genesis 3). As the Surgeon opens the wound, we see that there is not even one cell that is sound. "*There is no soundness in my flesh because of thine anger; neither is there any rest in my bones because of my sin. For mine iniquities are gone over mine head: as an heavy burden they are too heavy for me. My wounds stink and are corrupt because of my foolishness*" (Psalm 38:3-5). The more the Surgeon cuts away all hope in ourselves, death is the only thing possible for us. In our heart the thought arises, to die would be to miss that only comfort spoken of in the first question. The heart cries out in desperation.

QUESTION: 8. ARE WE THEN so corrupt that we are wholly incapable of doing any good, and inclined to all wickedness?

ANSWER: INDEED WE ARE; EXCEPT we are regenerated by the Spirit of God.

This is as bad as it gets! The Surgeon says, "*Set thine house in order: for thou shalt die, and not live*" (Isaiah 38:1b). Is this the end? Yes! In us it is. But! There is an exception, regeneration. This flesh must die, but in its death there is hope. "*That which is born of the flesh is flesh; and that which is born of the Spirit is spirit*" (John 3:6). It is a work that God, the Holy Ghost alone can do, "*Ye must be born again*" John 3:7b). To find the only comfort I become nothing and God becomes everything! This is why this surgery is necessary.

5.
The Natural Man Questions God

QUESTION: 9. DOTH NOT GOD then do injustice to man, by requiring from him in his law, that which he cannot perform?

ANSWER: NOT AT ALL; FOR God made man capable of performing it; but man; by the instigation of the devil, and his own willful disobedience, deprived himself and all his posterity of those divine gifts.

O, the wicked audacity of the human heart! *"Nay but, O man, who art thou that repliest against God? Shall the thing formed say to him that formed it, Why hast thou made me thus"* (Romans 9:20)? God has given us a ray of hope through His Word that the only way of escape is to be regenerated by the Holy Spirit, outside of himself. Man still wants to do something himself for his salvation. Man is unwilling to admit he is completely unable to help himself. He will admit he needs help, or a crutch for support, but does not need to lean on Him completely. This is the part of the flesh which must be rooted out. But why?

QUESTION: 10. Will God suffer such disobedience and rebellion to go unpunished?

ANSWER: By no means; but is terribly displeased with our original as well as actual sins; and will punish them in his just judgment temporally and eternally, as he hath declared, "Cursed is everyone that continueth not in all things, which are written in the book of the law, to do them.

Psalm 5:5, "*The foolish shall not stand in thy sight: thou hatest all workers of iniquity.*" Nothing that is not pure can stand in the presence of God. This is the object of the Divine Surgeon as He opens the wound, removing bit by bit everything that offends. "*For as many as are of the works of the law are under the curse: for it is written, Cursed is every one that continueth not in all things which are written in the book of the law to do them*" (Galatians 3:10).

QUESTION 11: Is not God then also merciful?

ANSWER: God is indeed merciful, but also just; therefore his justice requires, that sin which is committed against the most high majesty of God, be punished with extreme, that is, with everlasting punishment of body and soul.

This last question is used by the Divine Surgeon to show that nothing of or in man can be used to bring about healing. When the patient is made to see his utter inability, he becomes a beggar. "*Wherefore I abhor myself, and repent in dust and ashes*" (Job 42:6). All questioning of what the Surgeon is doing is stopped. "*That every mouth may be stopped, and all the world may become guilty before God*" (Romans 3:19b). The only question that is left is, "If

God is indeed merciful, how can this justice be satisfied?" That question will find an answer in the Triune God Himself! The stripping Surgeon reveals the Healing Physician as a humanly impossible necessity.

6.
Payment must be made by the Sinner or Another

QUESTION: 12. SINCE THEN, BY the righteous judgment of God, we deserve temporal and eternal punishment, is there no way by which we may escape that punishment, and be again received into favor?

ANSWER: GOD WILL HAVE HIS justice satisfied; and therefore we must make this full satisfaction, either by ourselves, or by another.

God, the Holy Spirit, as the Surgeon, has cut away all hope of a cure in ourselves and at the same time put the hope in our heart that there is a way of escape. We acknowledge our guilt and declare God righteous in our condemnation for our sin to the One offended. *"For I acknowledge my transgressions: and my sin is ever before me. Against thee, thee only, have I sinned, and done this evil in thy sight: that thou mightest be justified when thou speakest, and be clear when thou judgest"* (Psalm 51:3-4). This is the seed of saving faith. The wonderful working of the Spirit brings us to see our need through the Word. He gently opens the soul's eye for the Deliverer from our just deserved punishment. The woman with the issue of blood came to Jesus after she spent all that she had on the physicians, receiving no cure for her sickness. She believed that if she could but touch the hem of His garment she would be healed. Death was staring her in the face. She had heard about this Man who healed the sick, raised the dead, and gave sight to the blind, so in her desperate need she went and received healing. But she received more, He, Jesus said, "*Thy faith has made thee whole; go in peace, and be whole of thy plague*" (Mark 5:34b). God knows how to bring us to see that man can only bring temporary relief at best, but that will never stand up before Him. Our sins are infinite and we are finite, making it a necessity that we find our help outside of ourselves.

QUESTION: 13. CAN WE OURSELVES then make this satisfaction?

ANSWER: BY NO MEANS; BUT on the contrary we daily increase our debt.

No wonder that Isaiah prophesied to the people, "*But your iniquities have separated between you and your God, and your sins have hid his face from you, that he will not hear*" (Isaiah 59:2). This is a fearful thing. If God will not hear, then all hope is lost. In spite of the mounting mountains of our sins, God is greater than all our mountains. "*Behold, the LORD'S hand is not shortened, that it cannot save; neither his ear heavy, that it cannot hear*" (Isaiah 59:1). He is the only one able to help needy and helpless sinners. "*For he, (Jehovah) shall deliver the needy when he crieth; the poor also, and him that hath no helper. He shall spare the poor and needy, and shall save the souls of the needy*" (Psalm 72:12-13). Yes! Our Catechism teacher is leading us through the Word, to the one who took on Him our original and actual sins, nailing them to the Accursed Cross to become the Deliverer that we cannot do without.

7.
The Able Physician

QUESTION: 14. CAN THERE BE found anywhere, one, who is a mere creature, able to satisfy for us?

ANSWER: NONE; FOR, FIRST, GOD will not punish any other creature for the sin which man hath committed; and further, no mere creature can sustain the burden of God's eternal wrath against sin, so as to deliver others from it.

QUESTION: 15. WHAT SORT OF a mediator and deliverer then must we seek for?

ANSWER: FOR ONE WHO IS very man, and perfectly righteous; and yet more powerful than all creatures; that is one who is also very God.

The Bible records many human deliverers who God used to deliver people and nations, but there were occasions when they were unable to complete the task. They fell short because of sin. But God promised to send a deliverer whose name is

Jehovah, who will save His people from their sin. He is the Divine Physician, the One who is the only Physician capable of restoring spiritually dead souls into living, vibrant lovers of God. God's Deliverer is His only begotten Son, who though equal with the Father, became man to be able to be the mediator for fallen man. "*That they all may be one; as thou, Father, art in me, and I in thee, that they also may be one in us: that the world may believe that thou hast sent me*" (John 17:21). He (Jesus) by His Word and Spirit can and will heal His needy people, restoring them into fellowship with His Father as sons and daughters. He is not only the able Physician, but the healing Balm for them as well. "*Is there no balm in Gilead; is there no physician there*" (Jeremiah 8:22a)? He is the Physician that never makes a mistake in diagnosis saying, "*I am come that they might have life, and that they might have it more abundantly*" (John 10:10b). This God-Man, who by His Word created the world and everything in it, has all power in heaven and on earth so that all things work together for His glory.

> The heavens praise, O Lord, Thy wonders day and night;
> Thy saints on earth extol Thy faithfulness and might;
> Exultingly they ask: Who, Lord, within Thy dwelling,
> Who of the kings of earth, in carnal strength excelling,
> Can be compared with Thee, Jehovah great and glorious,
> In all Thy wise designs triumphant and victorious?

The hosts of heaven, O Lord, acclaim Thee Lord alone,
And greatly fear Thy Name 'bove all around Thy throne.
Who is there like to Thee, throughout this vast creation,
Jehovah, Lord of hosts, the God of our salvation,
Arrayed like Thee with power and faithfulness astounding,
Constraining saints to praise Thy wonderous grace abounding?

Psalter 422:3-4

8.
Jesus Salvation

QUESTION: 16. WHY MUST HE be very man, and also perfectly righteous?

ANSWER: BECAUSE THE JUSTICE OF God requires that the same human nature which hath sinned, should likewise make satisfaction for sin; and one who is himself a sinner, cannot satisfy for others.

QUESTION: 17. WHY MUST HE in one person be also very God?

ANSWER: THAT HE MIGHT, BY the power of his Godhead sustain in his human nature, the burden of God's wrath; and might obtain for and restore to us, righteousness and life.

Eternal death is the only complete payment that can be accepted to appease the wrath of the offended God. This eternal death would have to be experienced by every sinner without a substitute as all have sinned and come short of the glory of God.

"*Wherefore, as by one man sin entered into the world, and death by sin; and so death passed upon all men, for that all have sinned*" (Romans 5:12). A threefold death, temporal, spiritual, and eternal death was the only future for the entire human race. God, Himself, must take upon Himself our human nature without the pollution of sin through His birth and conception by the Holy Ghost, through the Virgin Mary becoming the Mediator for His people. "*And the angel answered and said unto her, The Holy Ghost shall come upon thee, and the power of the Highest shall overshadow thee: therefore also that holy thing which shall be born of thee shall be called the Son of God*" (Luke 1:35). Only the Son of God would qualify to make satisfaction for the sins of His people. "*For such an high priest became us, who is holy, harmless, undefiled, separate from sinners, and made higher than the heavens; Who needeth not daily, as those high priests, to offer up sacrifice, first for his own sins, and then for the people's: for this he did once, when he offered up himself*" (Hebrews 7:26-27). He was willing to lay down His life for them, and reconciling them unto Himself, revealed His great love for them. "*And this is the record, that God hath given to us eternal life, and this life is in his Son. He that hath the Son hath life; and he that hath not the Son of God hath not life*" (1 John 5:11-12).

O Lord my God, how manifold
Thy wondrous works which I behold;
And all Thy loving gracious thought
Thou hast bestowed on man;
To count Thy mercies I have sought,
but boundless is their span.

Not sacrifice delights the Lord,
But he who hears and keeps His word;
Thou gavest me to hear Thy will,
Thy law is in my heart;
I come the Scripture to fulfill,
glad tidings to impart.

Psalter 111:3-4

9.
The Mediator Revealed

QUESTION: 18. WHO THEN IS that Mediator, who is in one person both very God, and a real righteous man?

ANSWER: OUR LORD JESUS CHRIST: who of God is made unto us wisdom, and righteousness, and sanctification, and redemption.

QUESTION: 19. WHENCE KNOWEST THOU this?

ANSWER: FROM THE HOLY GOSPEL, which God himself revealed in Paradise; and afterwards published by the patriarchs and prophets, and represented by the sacrifices and other ceremonies of the law; and lastly, has fulfilled it by his only begotten Son.

This is He whom the prophets and saints looked for with holy anticipation that in the fulness of time would be born according to the promises of God. "*And the angel said unto her, Fear not, Mary: for thou hast found favour with God. And, behold, thou shalt conceive in thy womb, and bring forth a son, and shalt call his name JESUS. He shall be great, and shall be called the Son of the Highest: and the Lord God shall give unto him the throne of his father David: And he shall reign over the house of Jacob for ever; and of his kingdom there shall be no end*" (Luke 1:30-33). The Bible from Genesis to Revelation has made Him known in all His power and beauty. "*Concerning his Son Jesus Christ our Lord, which was made of the seed of David according to the flesh; By whom we have received grace and apostleship, for obedience to the faith among all nations, for his name; And declared to be the Son of God with power, according to the spirit of holiness, by the resurrection from the dead*" (Romans 1:3-5). Have you been drawn to Him? Is Jesus Christ your redeemer? Nothing else can give life. He is the Physician! He is the Balm! He is everything for this life, and for the life to come!

> Praise ye the Lord, His praise proclaim,
> and, O my soul, bless thou His Name;
> Yea, I will sound His praise abroad
> and ever bless the Lord my God.

> Trust not in man who soon must die,
> but on the living God rely;
> Most blest the man whose help is
> He that made the heav's and earth and sea.

> His truth unchanged shall ever stand,
> He saves from strong oppression's hand
> in Him the sad a helper find,
> He feeds the poor and heals the blind.

Thy God shall reign forever more,
praise Him, O Zion, and adore;
The Lord is heav'n's eternal King,
to Him all praise and honor bring.

Psalter 401 taken from Psalm 146

10.
Salvation by True Faith

QUESTION: 20. ARE ALL MEN then, as they perished in Adam, saved by Christ?

ANSWER: No; ONLY THOSE WHO are ingrafted into Him, and receive all His benefits, by a true faith.

QUESTION: 21. WHAT IS TRUE faith?

ANSWER: TRUE FAITH IS NOT only a certain knowledge, whereby I hold for truth all that God has revealed to us in his word, but also an assured confidence, which the Holy Ghost works by the gospel, in my heart; that not only to others, but to me also, remission of sin, everlasting righteousness and salvation, are freely given by God, merely of grace, only for the sake of Christ's merits.

In Adam, all men die a spiritual death which is their just due, and God justly could have left them there. But God from eternity past had set apart a people, (the elect) for His glory.

He works this by sending the Word out to all, but as it goes out the Holy Spirit opens the heart of a person to receive the word. *"For by grace are ye saved through faith; and that not of yourselves: it is the gift of God: Not of works, lest any man should boast"* (Ephesians 2:8-9). Faith is implanted in their hearts by the Spirit upon hearing the Word. *"He came unto his own, and his own received him not. But as many as received him, to them gave he power to become the sons of God, even to them that believe on his name: Which were born, not of blood, nor of the will of the flesh, nor of the will of man, but of God"* (John 1:11-13). As God's Word is proclaimed and the convicted sinner cries out for mercy the Divine Physician hears the cry and applies the healing balm to the dying soul. *"And a certain woman named Lydia, a seller of purple, of the city of Thyatira, which worshipped God, heard us: whose heart the Lord opened, that she attended unto the things which were spoken of Paul"* (Acts 16:14). *"Salvation is of the Lord"* (Jonah 2:9b).

The wonder of salvation is that it is not about man, it ends in the glory of the Triune God of love. The most vivid picture of that is at the Hill Calvary, to the world a despised place, but for His elect their garment of salvation was woven in His precious blood! *"I am crucified with Christ: nevertheless I live; yet not I, but Christ liveth in me: and the life which I now live in the flesh I live by the faith of the Son of God, who loved me, and gave himself for me"* (Galatians 2:20). This fills the heart with a confidence that even though it seems too good to be true our faith is in Him and His finished work. *"Now faith is the substance of things hoped for, the evidence of things not seen"* (Hebrews 11:1). The more

His love fills our heart, the more we seek to know Him and everything about Him. With all our hearts we say, "I believe that Jesus Christ died for me!" *"For as many as are led by the Spirit of God, they are the sons of God. For ye have not received the spirit of bondage again to fear; but ye have received the Spirit of adoption, whereby we cry, Abba, Father. The Spirit itself beareth witness with our spirit, that we are the children of God: And if children, then heirs; heirs of God, and joint-heirs with Christ; if so be that we suffer with him, that we may be also glorified together"* (Romans 8:14-17). Salvation is a personal experience, with personal pronouns! Has Jesus Christ by faith set you free?

11.
Righteousness through the Gospel Promises

QUESTION: 22. WHAT IS THEN necessary for a Christian to believe?

ANSWER: ALL THINGS PROMISED US in the gospel, which the articles of our catholic undoubted Christian faith briefly teach us.

QUESTION: 23. WHAT ARE THESE articles?

ANSWER:

1. I believe in God the Father, Almighty, Maker of heaven and earth:
2. And in Jesus Christ, His only begotten Son, our Lord:
3. Who was conceived by the Holy Ghost, born of the Virgin Mary:
4. Suffered under Pontius Pilate; was crucified, dead, and buried: He descended into hell:

5. The third day He rose again from the dead:
6. He ascended into heaven, and sitteth at the right hand of God the Father Almighty:
7. From thence He shall come to judge the quick and the dead:
8. I believe in the Holy Ghost:
9. I believe an holy catholic church: the communion of saints:
10. The forgiveness of sins:
11. The resurrection of the body:
12. And the life everlasting. AMEN.

Having learned who could be the only Mediator for fallen man, and fallen in love with Him, we need to know how we are to worship Him. We are social creatures so that to love Him we need to know what He would expect of us. "*If ye love me, keep my commandments*" (John 14:15) Jesus told His followers. This is the thread which runs through the whole Bible. But more than that we also need to know who this God-man is, and this is made known in the Apostles Creed. "*Show me thy ways, O LORD; teach me thy paths*" (Psalm 25:4). Knowing and understanding this causes us to bow in adoration before Him. We exalt Him in humility, and increase our love for Him. As we search out these twelve articles we, like the queen of Sheba will cry out, "*Howbeit I believed not their words, until I came, and mine eyes had seen it: and, behold, the one half of the greatness of thy wisdom was not told me: for thou exceedest the fame that I heard*" (2 Chronicles 9:6). May this be our experience as we search the Word of God! He will become exceeding precious to us so that we would tell others about our great God. "*Oh that men would praise the LORD for his goodness, and for his wonderful works to the children of men! Let them exalt him also in the congregation of the people, and praise him in the assembly of the elders*" (Psalm 107:31-32). God is known among His people! "*So will I make my holy name known in the midst of my people Israel; and I will not let them pollute my holy name any more: and the heathen shall know that I am the LORD, the Holy One in Israe*l" (Ezekiel 39:7).

12.
How Is God to be Believed

QUESTION: 24. How are these articles divided?

ANSWER: Into three parts; the first is of God the Father and our creation; the second of God the Son and our redemption; the third, of God the Holy Ghost and our sanctification.

QUESTION: 25. Since there is but one only divine essence, why speakest thou of Father, Son, and Holy Ghost?

ANSWER: Because God hath so revealed Himself in his word, that these three distinct persons are the one only true and eternal God.

God is to be believed as the Word of truth. There are many truths which are hard to be understood, but that should not be a problem. God always was. "*In the beginning God created the heaven and the earth. And the earth was without form, and void; and darkness was upon the face of the deep. And the Spirit of God moved upon the face of the waters. And God said, Let there be light: and there was light. "* (Genesis 1:1-3). The Bible begins by revealing the Triune God, the Father created, and the Son (the Word) spoke it into being, and the Holy Ghost moved on the face of the waters. This must be believed for salvation to be possible. God is one in essence, three in personalities, fully satisfied and complete in Himself not needing anything besides. This is the God we worship, serve, and adore! There is salvation in none other, because there is none other! To not believe His Word is the ultimate sin. "*Jesus said unto them, If God were your Father, ye would love me: for I proceeded forth and came from God; neither came I of myself, but he sent me. Why do ye not understand my speech? even because ye cannot hear my word. Ye are of your father the devil, and the lusts of your father ye will do. He was a murderer from the beginning, and abode not in the truth, because there is no truth in him. When he speaketh a lie, he speaketh of his own: for he is a liar, and the father of it. And because I tell you the truth, ye believe me not*" (John 8:42-45). But to those, who by grace believe His word, shall be saved. "Then said Jesus to those Jews which believed on him, If ye continue in my word, then are ye my disciples indeed; And ye shall know the truth, and the truth shall make you free" (John 8:31-32).

Doxology
To Father, Son, and Holy Ghost,
The God, whom heav'ns triumphant host,
And saints on earth adore;
Be glory as in ages past,
And now it is, and so shall last,
When time shall be no more.

13.
Of God the Father

QUESTION: 26. WHAT BELIEVEST THOU when thou sayest, "I believe in God the Father, Almighty, Maker of heaven and earth"?

ANSWER: THAT THE ETERNAL FATHER of our Lord Jesus Christ (who of nothing made heaven and earth, with all that is in them; who likewise upholds and governs the same by His eternal council and providence) is for the sake of Christ his Son, my God and my Father; on whom I rely so entirely, that I have no doubt, but He will provide me with all things necessary for soul and body: and further, that He will make whatever evils He sends upon me, in this valley of tears turn out to my advantage; for He is able to do it, being Almighty God, and willing being a faithful Father.

A father to us is one who is head of the family. The family looks up to the father for advice and direction. It is so even in the Trinity. "*But that the world may know that I love the Father; and as the Father gave me commandment, even so I do. Arise, let us go hence*" (John 14:31). In the Trinity none is greater than the other, and yet Jesus Christ is the Son of the Father and the Spirit proceeds from them both, yet only one God. "*But I would have you know, that the head of every man is Christ; and the head of the woman is the man; and the head of Christ is God*" (1 Corinthians 11:3). This is a mystery way above the ability of our minds to comprehend.

The Father governs and directs all things for His glory and our good. "*And we know that all things work together for good to them that love God, to them who are the called according to his purpose*" (Romans 8:28). He is King of kings and no one can say, "What doeth thou?" "*The LORD hath prepared his throne in the heavens; and his kingdom ruleth over all*" Psalm 103:19). The world continues day by day under His direction, leading His chosen people through this world to their eternal home which is the Fathers house. Everything may seem to be out of control, but it is not! He (the Father) is the Almighty God whose mercy never faileth.

Established in the highest heav'ns the Lord has set His throne,
And over all His kingdom rules, for He is God alone.
Psalter 279:1 taken from Psalm 103

14.
The Providence of God

QUESTION: 27. WHAT DOST THOU mean by the providence of God?

ANSWER: THE ALMIGHTY AND EVERYWHERE present power of God; whereby, as it were by his hand, he upholds and governs heaven and earth, and all creatures; so that herbs and grass, rain and draught, fruitful and barren years, meat and drink, health and sickness, riches and poverty, yea, and all things come not by chance, but by His fatherly hand.

QUESTION: 28. WHAT ADVANTAGE IS it to us to know that God has created, and by His providence doth still uphold all things?

ANSWER: THAT WE MAY BE patient in adversity; thankful in prosperity; and that in all things, which may hereafter befall us, we place our firm trust in our faithful God and Father, that nothing shall separate us from His love; since all creatures are so in His hand, that without His will they cannot so much as move.

The root word of providence is to provide for. Fathers provide for the needs of their families to the best of their abilities, but may fall short because of circumstances beyond their control. Our best intentions many times are failures, but there is one God the Father. He never fails, His promises are sure. Both the wicked and the righteous benefit for this life. God's provisions are inexhaustible, His power is unlimited, and His mercy and grace is greater than the highest mountain of our sins. *"In whom we have redemption through his blood, the forgiveness of sins, according to the riches of his grace; Wherein he hath abounded toward us in all wisdom and prudence; Having made known unto us the mystery of his will, according to his good pleasure which he hath purposed in himself"* (Ephesians 1:7-9). God, who spoke the world into being, *"Upholding all things by the Word of His power"* (Hebrews 1:3). Evil had no power over Him, but He overcame the world. *"These things I have spoken unto you, that in me ye might have peace. In the world ye shall have tribulation: but be of good cheer; I have overcome the world"* (John 16:33). This is the strength of God's poor and powerless people as they receive their strength from Him. They find Him, in their extremities, always faithful and true. His love never changes, He loved them from before the world was. He loved them in time while they were enemies. He shows His love for them by sending His Son to the cross for them, and He loves them with an eternal love. He made them thankful to Him no matter what came upon them. They have learned that they deserve nothing, but have received everything. *"Blessed be the God and Father of our Lord Jesus Christ, which according to his abundant mercy hath begotten us again unto a lively hope by the resurrection of Jesus Christ from the dead, To an inheritance incorruptible, and undefiled, and that fadeth not away, reserved in heaven for you, Who are kept by the power of God through faith unto salvation ready to be revealed in the last time"* (1 Peter 1:3-5).

15.
Jesus the Son of God

QUESTION: 29. WHY IS THE Son of God called Jesus, that is a Savior?

ANSWER: BECAUSE HE SAVETH US, and delivereth us from our sins; and likewise, because we ought not to seek, neither can find salvation in any other.

QUESTION: 30. DO SUCH THEN believe in Jesus the only Savior, who seek their salvation and welfare of saints, of themselves, or anywhere else?

ANSWER: THEY DO NOT; FOR though they boast of him in words yet in deeds they deny Jesus the only deliverer and Savior; for one of these two things must be true, that either Jesus is not a complete Savior; or that they, who by a true faith receive this Savior, must find all things in him necessary to their salvation.

The time for the long awaited deliverer had come! *"For yet a little while, and he that shall come will come, and will not tarry"*

(Hebrews 10:37). All the types and figures of the Old Testament pointed to this point in history. "*And she shall bring forth a son, and thou shalt call his name JESUS: for he shall save his people from their sins*" (Matthew 1:21). Jesus is an exclusive Name. God cannot be approached but by the Name of Jesus. "*Neither is there salvation in any other: for there is none other name under heaven given among men, whereby we must be saved*" (Acts 4:12). The Name of Jesus is hated by the world. This can be seen by the world's hatred of His people. "*If the world hate you, ye know that it hated me before it hated you. If ye were of the world, the world would love his own: but because ye are not of the world, but I have chosen you out of the world, therefore the world hateth you*" (John 15:18-19). God's love for His people is revealed in His Son, (Jesus). "*Beloved, believe not every spirit, but try the spirits whether they are of God: because many false prophets are gone out into the world. Hereby know ye the Spirit of God: Every spirit that confesseth that Jesus Christ is come in the flesh is of God: And every spirit that confesseth not that Jesus Christ is come in the flesh is not of God: and this is that spirit of antichrist, whereof ye have heard that it should come; and even now already is it in the world*" (1 John 4:1-3). The Name of Jesus is precious to His people because He is their life.

How sweet the name of Jesus sounds in a believer's ear;
It soothes his sorrows, heals his wounds, and drives away his fear.

It makes the wounded spirit whole and calms the troubled breast;
'Tis manna to the hungry soul and to the weary rest.

Dear name! the rock on which I build, my shield and hiding place;
My never failing treasure, filled with boundless stores of grace!

Jesus, my Shepherd, Brother, Friend, my Prophet, Priest and King,
My Lord, my Life, my Way, my End, accept the praise I bring.

Till then I would Thy love proclaim with ev'ry fleeting breath;
And may the music of Thy name refresh my soul in death.

Mr. John Newton

16.
The Christ of God

QUESTION: 31. WHY IS HE called Christ, that is anointed?

ANSWER: BECAUSE HE IS ORDAINED of God the Father, and anointed with the Holy Ghost, to be our chief Prophet and Teacher, who has fully revealed to us the secret counsel and will of God concerning our redemption; and to be our only High Priest who by the sacrifice of His body, has redeemed us, and makes continual intercession with the Father for us; and also to be our eternal King, who governs us by His word and Spirit, and who defends and preserves us in (the enjoyment of) that salvation, He has purchased for us.

QUESTION: 32. BUT WHY ART thou called a Christian?

ANSWER: BECAUSE I AM A member of Christ by faith, and thus am partaker of His anointing; that so I may confess His name and present myself a living sacrifice of thankfulness to him; and also that with a free and good conscience I may fight against sin and Satan in this life: and afterwards reign with him eternally, over all creatures.

"*Therefore let no man glory in men. For all things are yours; Whether Paul, or Apollos, or Cephas, or the world, or life, or death, or things present, or things to come; all are yours; And ye are Christ's; and Christ is God's*" (1 Corinthians 3:21-23). The Name of Christ signifies Ruler, Protector, and Lord over all, yet always working to do the will of His Father. "*And he said unto them,* (Mary his mother and Joseph) *How is it that ye sought me? wist ye not that I must be about my Father's business*" (Luke 2:49). His Father's business is to build His kingdom by His Word and Spirit renewing lost and hell bound sinners to His image again. "*I am come that they might have life, and that they might have it more abundantly*" (John 10:10b). The Word of Christ is powerful nothing can resist it, even death flees from Him. "*For he spake, and it was done; he commanded, and it stood fast*" (Psalm 33:9).

Christ draws sinners to Himself by filling them with His love and they follow Him as He reveals Himself to them. "*But as many as received him, to them gave he power to become the sons of God, even to them that believe on his name: Which were born, not of blood, nor of the will of the flesh, nor of the will of man, but of God. And the Word was made flesh, and dwelt among us, (and we beheld his glory, the glory as of the only begotten of the Father,) full of grace and truth*" (John 1:12-14). For this He (Christ) must be Almighty, purchasing salvation for them through the shedding of His blood on the cross. The world views the cross as weakness, but it stands as a emblem of strength for them. He arose and is now seated at the right hand of power defending and preserving

His church for Himself. "*All power is given unto me in heaven and in earth*" (Matthew 28:18b). To be a "Christian" takes on a whole new meaning. To not follow this Christ would be to lose the only One who has loved me and gave Himself for me. To follow Him is eternal life and to live for Him forever, which is what we were created for. Will You follow Him?

17.
The Only Begotten Son of God, Our Lord

QUESTION: 33. WHY IS CHRIST called the only begotten Son of God, since we are also the children of God?

ANSWER: BECAUSE CHRIST ALONE IS the eternal and natural Son of God; but we are children adopted of God, by grace for His sake.

QUESTION: 34. WHEREFORE CALLEST THOU Him our Lord?

ANSWER: BECAUSE HE HATH REDEEMED us, both soul and body, from all our sins, not with gold or silver, but with His precious blood, and hath delivered us from all the power of the devil; and thus hath made us His own property.

Jesus Christ, who said to His disciples of Himself, "*I and my Father are one*" (John 10:30). God's people are called His children, but it cannot be said that we are equal or one with Him in His Divine nature. As His created beings, we are sons and daughters in Jesus Christ, but He is the divine Son of the Father.

He took on Him our human flesh. As God there were two natures in one. "*And the Word was made flesh, and dwelt among us, (and we beheld his glory, the glory as of the only begotten of the Father,) full of grace and truth*" (John 1:14). This is a glorious mystery which will take an eternity to fully know the height, depth, and width of the truth. He is the only eternal, only begotten Son of God, but in that capacity He is our LORD also. "*And David himself saith in the book of Psalms, The Lord said unto my Lord, Sit thou on my right hand, Till I make thine enemies thy footstool*" (Luke 20:42-43).

As Our Lord, He is not only my Brother, but my Redeemer King! The world views Him only as a good man who died a martyr's death at best, but His people behold His death as their life, His cross as their security and refuge. Satan, the enemy of Christ and His church, was defeated there forever. "*Forasmuch as ye know that ye were not redeemed with corruptible things, as silver and gold, from your vain conversation received by tradition from your fathers; But with the precious blood of Christ, as of a lamb without blemish and without spot: Who verily was foreordained before the foundation of the world, but was manifest in these last times for you, Who by him do believe in God, that raised him up from the dead, and gave him glory; that your faith and hope might be in God*" (1 Peter 1:18-21). This gave Him ownership of all His elect having received from the Father a receipt (Paid in full). Yes! As the Only Begotten Son of God I own Him as mine only, for the sake of His merits, and am willing take Him as my Lord. "*For ye are bought with a price: therefore glorify God in your body, and in your spirit, which are God's*" (1 Corinthians 6:20).

18.
The Approachable Savior

QUESTION: 35. WHAT IS THE meaning of these words---"He was conceived by the Holy Ghost, born of the Virgin Mary"?

ANSWER: THAT GOD'S ETERNAL SON, who is, and continueth true and eternal God took upon Him the very nature of man, of the flesh and blood of the Virgin Mary, by the operation of the Holy Ghost; that He might also be the true seed of David, like unto His brethren in all things, sin excepted.

QUESTION: 36. WHAT PROFIT DOST thou receive by Christ's holy conception and nativity?

ANSWER: THAT HE IS OUR Mediator: and with His innocence and perfect holiness, covers in the sight of God, my sins wherein I was conceived and brought forth.

Citizens of a country get excited when their President or Ruler announces he will be coming to the city where they live. The whole city is abuzz and they all try to be in position to catch a glimpse or even say a word to him. But for the most part there is disappointment, He is not approachable. However in the fulness of time when God sent His son into the world, He sent an angel to a poor virgin girl; not to the palace to be born a prince, where all that would, could come to be received by Him. Angels were sent to announce the birth to shepherds in the field. Jesus came not for the righteous, but for poor and needy sinners, not only to be approachable, but to seek out His sheep.. He, (Jesus Christ the Son of God), Creator of heaven and earth took on Him the nature of fallen man. *"Who, being in the form of God, thought it not robbery to be equal with God: But made himself of no reputation, and took upon him the form of a servant, and was made in the likeness of men: And being found in fashion as a man, he humbled himself, and became obedient unto death, even the death of the cross"* (Philippians 2:6-8). We were conceived in sin, inherited from our father Adam due to disobedience in Paradise. We forfeited all rights in ourselves to be reconciled to God. *"For we have not an high priest which cannot be touched with the feeling of our infirmities; but was in all points tempted like as we are, yet without sin"* (Hebrews 4:15). But Jesus, the Mediator, was conceived by the Holy Ghost, born of the Virgin Mary as the second Adam without sin to make a way by the shedding of His blood for all His people. *"In whom we have redemption through his blood, the forgiveness of sins, according to the riches of his grace; Wherein he hath abounded toward us in all wisdom and prudence; Having made known unto us the mystery of his will, according to his good pleasure which he hath purposed in himself"* (Ephesians 1:7-9).

This is the glad tidings of the gospel, the Good News for lost sinners. What a wonderful Mediator who when they come to Him, will not only get a glimpse of Him but He speaks words of peace to them! *"Wherefore I say unto thee, Her sins, which are many, are forgiven; for she loved much: but to whom little is forgiven, the same loveth little. And he said unto her, Thy sins are forgiven"* (Luke 7:47-48). This King of kings says, *"All power is given unto me in heaven and earth"* (Matthew 28:18b). There is no profit in anything else but in Him alone. Yes! He is approachable as the God-man Savior!

19.
The Suffering Savior

QUESTION: 37. WHAT DOST THOU understand by the words, "He suffered"?

ANSWER: THAT HE, ALL THE time that He lived on earth, but especially at the end of His life, sustained in body and soul, the wrath of God against the sins of all mankind: that so His passion as the only propitiatory sacrifice, he might redeem our body and soul from everlasting damnation, and obtain for us the favor of God, righteousness, and eternal life.

To begin to understand the suffering that had to be endured by the God-man Mediator we need to properly understand who He is that is enduring the suffering and who is the cause of all this suffering. Man has sinned against His Creator who is infinite, thereby requiring an infinite payment. Man had not only sinned, but with every breath he only adds to the sin. For man who is finite to pay an infinite penalty could never be done. The mountain of this sin, by us, would never become smaller, but only increases and this is only for one man. The Bible says that 'all have sinned'. Jesus came to this world to suffer and die for sins He had not committed. The sins of the world were being carried by Him. These sins could not be passed by. The cross, as cruel a punishment as it was, was not the real weight that was crushing Christ, but the wrath of God against sin. As the Lord's supper form says, "The He (Jesus) assumed our flesh and blood; that he bore for us the wrath of God (under which we would have perished everlastingly) from the beginning of His incarnation, to the end of his life upon earth; and that he had fulfilled, for us all obedience to the divine law, and righteousness; especially, when the weight of our sins pressed out of him the bloody sweat in the garden, where he was bound that we might be freed from our sins." To begin to see this, He becomes precious to His people because it was all love for them. *"Forasmuch as ye know that ye were not redeemed with corruptible things, as silver and gold, from your vain conversation received by tradition from your fathers; But with the precious blood of Christ, as of a lamb without blemish and without spot: Who verily was foreordained before the foundation of the world, but was manifest in these last times for you, Who by him do believe in God, that raised him up from the dead, and gave him glory; that your faith and hope might be in God"* 1 Peter 1:18-21). This, according to His word, he did with delight! *"Then said I, Lo, I come: in the volume of the book it is written of me, I delight to do thy will, O my God: yea, thy law is within my heart"* (Psalm 40: 7-8). Eternity is blessed because of this great and precious doctrine of divine love for hell-worthy sinners, made white in the blood of the Suffering Savior! Why did He love His people so? There is only one reason! BECAUSE HE LOVES US!

20.
The Innocent Declared Guilty

QUESTION: 38. WHY DID HE suffer under Pontius Pilate, as judge?

ANSWER: THAT HE BEING INNOCENT, and yet condemned by a temporal judge, might thereby free us from the severe judgment of God to which we were exposed.

QUESTION: 39. IS THERE ANYTHING more in His being crucified, than if he had died some other death?

ANSWER: YES (THERE IS); FOR thereby I am assured, that He took on Him the curse which lay upon me; for the death of the cross was accursed of God.

Jesus Christ came into the world to die, the just for the unjust, in this the sovereignty of God is shown in vivid colors. Jesus, let Pontius Pilate as the earthly judge know this, "*Thou couldest have no power at all against me, except it were given thee from above: therefore he that delivered me unto thee hath the greater sin*" (John

19:11b). Three times Pilate responded, "I find no fault in this man," as recorded in all four gospels and yet He condemned Him to be crucified, and set the most evil of criminals free. This is the wonder of <u>free and sovereign grace</u>, Him for me! Barabbas's go free, Jesus takes their place! "*What if God, willing to show his wrath, and to make his power known, endured with much longsuffering the vessels of wrath fitted to destruction: And that he might make known the riches of his glory on the vessels of mercy, which he had afore prepared unto glory, Even us, whom he hath called, not of the Jews only, but also of the Gentiles*" (Romans 9:22-24)? He bore the wrath of God; we bask in the joy of the Lord! "*O the depth of the riches both of the wisdom and knowledge of God! how unsearchable are his judgments, and his ways past finding out*" (Romans 11:33)! Yes! This is the heart of God exposed in all its <u>love in majesty</u>, glorifying His Triune Name through His only begotten Son, Jesus Christ our Lord. What think ye of Jesus Christ?

O praise ye the Lord and sing a new song, amid all His saints His praises prolong; the praise of their Maker His people shall sing, And children of Zion rejoice in their King.

With timbrel and harp and joyful acclaim, with gladness and mirth, Sing praise to His Name; for God in His people His pleasure doth seek, With robes of salvation He clotheth the meek. Psalter 407:1-2 taken from Psalm 149

21.
The Dying Savior

QUESTION: 40. WHY WAS IT necessary for Christ to humble Himself even unto death?

ANSWER: BECAUSE WITH RESPECT TO the justice and truth of God, satisfaction for our sins could be made no otherwise, than by the death of the Son of God.

QUESTION: 41. WHY WAS HE also buried?

ANSWER: THEREBY TO PROVE THAT He was really dead.

QUESTION: 42. SINCE THEN CHRIST died for us why must we also die?

ANSWER: OUR DEATH IS NOT a satisfaction for our sins, but only an abolishing of sin, and a passing into eternal life.

The justice of God can only be satisfied by Christ, nothing less will do. This is the answer to question and answer 12, "God will have His justice satisfied; and therefore we must make this full satisfaction, either by ourselves, or by another." Christ as the Substitute could not only come to this earth as a perfectly holy man, but must pay the extreme penalty due to us, which was death. "*Thou hast loved righteousness, and hated iniquity; therefore God, even thy God, hath anointed thee with the oil of gladness above thy fellows*" (Hebrews 1:9). Without this there could not be any forgiveness and reconciliation to God. "*Christ died for our sins according to the scriptures*" (1 Corinthians 15:3b). With death there must be a burial; this gives proof of death and closure to the family of the loved ones. But, this death also has a comforting dimension as Christ died for the sins of His people; our sins were buried with Him never to be remembered anymore. "*Verily, verily, I say unto you, He that heareth my word, and believeth on him that sent me, hath everlasting life, and shall not come into condemnation; but is passed from death unto life*" (John 5:24). This was experienced by the thief on the cross in a very dramatic way, but all of God's children learn this as their justification before God. "*But God commendeth his love toward us, in that, while we were yet sinners, Christ died for us. Much more then, being now justified by his blood, we shall be saved from wrath through him*" (Romans 5:8-9). O, the depth of the love of a Triune God, who would give His only, begotten Son to the accursed death of the cross to reconcile enemies and rebels into friends and family. "*O the depth of the riches both of the wisdom and knowledge of God! how unsearchable are his judgments, and his ways past finding out*" (Romans 11:33)! Yes! He died, and was buried and with it all our sins; this is not the end but the beginning as Jesus said, "*I give unto them eternal life; and they shall never perish, neither shall any man pluck them out of my hand*" (John 10:28). We shall see this dying Savior is the living Savior, and with Him all His people shall live too!

The Church's one foundation is Jesus Christ her Lord;
She is His new creation by water and the Word:
From heav'n He came and sought her to be His holy bride;
With His own blood He bought her, and for her life He died.
Hymn by Samuel J. Stone

22.
Corruption Crucified and Buried

QUESTION: 43. WHAT FURTHER BENEFIT do we receive from the sacrifice and death of Christ?

ANSWER: THAT BY VIRTUE THEREOF, our old man is crucified, dead and buried with Him; that so the inclination of the flesh may no more reign in us; but that we may offer ourselves unto Him a sacrifice of thanksgiving.

QUESTION: 44. WHY IS IT added, "He descended into hell"?

ANSWER: THAT IN MY GREATEST temptations, I may be assured, and wholly comfort myself in this, that my Lord Jesus Christ, by his inexpressible anguish, pains, terrors, and hellish agonies, in which He was plunged during all His sufferings, but especially on the cross hath delivered me from the anguish and torments of hell.

The plague of God's people is the corruption of sin in their bodies. The more they look to Christ the more they would be holy; without sin like Him. This is His promise to them, but they see so much corruption left inside and the cry bursts out, *"O wretched man that I am! who shall deliver me from the body of this death"* (Romans 7:24)? He (the Holy Spirit) brings them to the cross of Jesus and we look in wonder at Him who shed His blood for such a wretch as me, confessing our sin! *"If we confess our sins, he is faithful and just to forgive us our sins, and to cleanse us from all unrighteousness"* (1 John 1:9). The answer to what the Surgeon did as He cut away everything of us, filling the void with Himself, becomes too much for our poor human body to bear. Love of this Savior, Jesus Christ, overwhelms us so that with heart, soul, and mind we cry out with the Hymnist, William Featherston

> "My Jesus I love Thee, I know Thou are mine
> for Thee all the follies of sin I resign;
> My gracious Redeemer, my Savior art Thou:
> I ever I loved Thee, my Jesus 'tis now.
> I love Thee because thou hast first loved me
> And purchased my pardon on Calvary's tree;
> I love Thee for wearing the thorns on Thy brow:
> If ever I love Thee, my Jesus 'tis now.

He took the hell His church deserved conquering it for them. *"Now before the feast of the passover, when Jesus knew that his hour was come that he should depart out of this world unto the Father, having loved his own which were in the world, he loved them unto the end"* (John 13:1). The world with everything in it is of no value and Jesus becomes everything. The question, what further benefit do we receive from Him? O! It is a benefit which will never end, but bring praise, honor, and glory to Him forever. Are these benefits yours?

23.
He Is Risen

QUESTION: 45. WHAT DOES THE resurrection of Christ profit us?

ANSWER: FIRST, BY HIS RESURRECTION he has overcome death, that He might make us partakers of that righteousness which He had purchased for us by his death, secondly, we are also by His power raised up to a new life; and lastly, the resurrection of Christ is a sure pledge of our blessed resurrection.

We have seen that the sufferings, death, and burial of the Lord Jesus Christ was necessary as a new beginning for sinners, in them the new birth is signified. There must be a resurrection. New life must begin. *"For if the dead rise not, then is not Christ raised: And if Christ be not raised, your faith is vain; ye are yet in your sins"* 1 Corinthian 15:16). It is the greeting of a new day, a new chapter in our life. *"Therefore if any man be in Christ, he is a new creature: old things are passed away; behold, all things are become new"* (2 Corinthians 5:17). For God's people the resurrection is God's guarantee that the payment Christ made was accepted as full payment for all the sins of His people by His Father. *"There is therefore now no condemnation to them which are in Christ Jesus, who walk not after the flesh, but after the Spirit. For the law of the Spirit of life in Christ Jesus hath made me free from the law of sin and death"* (Romans 8:1-2). This gives courage and strength to walk through the world as strangers and pilgrims, knowing in spite of your doubts and fears, we are secure in Him. *"And if Christ be in you, the body is dead because of sin; but the Spirit is life because of righteousness. But if the Spirit of him that raised up Jesus from the dead dwell in you, he that raised up Christ from the dead shall also quicken your mortal bodies by his Spirit that dwelleth in you. Therefore, brethren, we are debtors, not to the flesh, to live after the flesh. For if ye live after the flesh, ye shall die: but if ye through the Spirit do mortify the deeds of the body, ye shall live. For as many as are led by the Spirit of God, they are the sons of God"* (Romans 8:11-14). We should with the saints of old greet each other, *"The Lord is risen indeed"* (Luke 24:34b). The resurrection brought two different reactions. The glory of the Lord brought fear and terror in the guards who became like dead men and ran away. But the women came though fearful yet they were drawn by love and were comforted by the angels who said, *"He is not here, but is risen"* Luke 24:6a). Jesus is ever mindful of His people and will meet them in the way! Which way are you following?

Now let the heav'ns be joyful! Let earth her song begin!
The world resound in triumph, and all that is therein:
Let all things seen and unseen their notes of gladness blend;
For Christ the Lord hath risen, Our Joy that hath no end.
Hymn by John of Damascus

24.
The King's Homecoming

QUESTION: 46. How DOST THOU understand these words, "He ascended into heaven?

ANSWER: That Christ, in sight of His disciples, was taken up from earth into heaven; and that He continues there for our interest, until He comes again to judge the quick and the dead.

QUESTION: 47. Is not Christ then with us even to the end of the world, as He promised?

ANSWER: Christ is very man and very God; with respect to His human nature, He is no more on earth; but with respect to His Godhead, majesty, grace and spirit, He is at no time absent from us.

Jesus after He rose from the grave comforted Mary. "*Touch me not; for I am not yet ascended to my Father: but go to my brethren, and say unto them, I ascend unto my Father, and your Father; and to my God, and your God*" (John 20:17). He had finished the work of redemption made necessary by the failure of the first Adam, necessitating His coming in the flesh for the salvation of His elect in the fulness of time. "*I have glorified thee on the earth: I have finished the work which thou gavest me to do. And now, O Father, glorify thou me with thine own self with the glory which I had with thee before the world was*" John 17:4-5). The stage was set for Christ as the victorious conquering King, to return to glory with His Fathers blessing, showing Him all the trophies of His conquest, but also to be the interceding High Priest for them continually before the Father. And as Prophet, Christ sends His Spirit to witness to them of Himself that they are the sons of God. "*For as many as are led by the Spirit of God, they are the sons of God*" (Romans 8:14).

His ascension gives hope for His people that He will do as He has said, "*In my Father's house are many mansions: if it were not so, I would have told you. I go to prepare a place for you. And if I go and prepare a place for you, I will come again, and receive you unto myself; that where I am, there ye may be also*" (John 14:2-3). Yes! Jesus Christ will come to judge the world in righteousness. The only righteousness that will stand on that day is the bloody righteousness which He earned for His people at His first coming. He came as a babe in Bethlehem, humbled Himself even to the death on the cross, conquered death and hell for His people, fulfilling all the promises in His Word. He will come again, but this time in all His glory and majesty on the clouds of heaven. Are you looking for Him?

O Lord, Thou hast ascended on high in might to reign;
Captivity Thou leadest a captive in Thy train,
Rich gifts to Thee are offered by men who did rebel,
Who pray that now Jehovah their God with them may dwell.

All glory might and honor ascribe to God on high;
His arm protects His people, who on His pow'r rely,
Forth from Thy holy dwelling Thy awful glories shine;
Thou strengthenedst Thy people; unending praise be Thine.

Psalter 183:1and4

25.
The God-man in Heaven

QUESTION: 48. BUT IF HIS human nature is not present, wherever His Godhead is, are then these two natures in Christ separated from one another?

ANSWER: NOT AT ALL, FOR since the Godhead is illimitable and omnipresent, it must necessarily follow that the same is beyond the limits of the human nature He assumed, and yet is nevertheless in this human nature, and remains personally united to it.

QUESTION: 49. OF WHAT ADVANTAGE to us is Christ's ascension into heaven?

ANSWER: FIRST, THAT HE IS our advocate in the presence of His Father in heaven; secondly, that we have flesh in heaven as a sure pledge that He, as the head, will also take up to Himself, us, His members; thirdly, that he sends us His Spirit as an earnest, by whose power we "seek the things which are above, where

Christ sitteth on the right hand of God and not things on earth."

God spoke the world into being, and upholds it by the word of His power. Our human mind cannot comprehend divine things, let alone God whom even the heaven of heavens cannot contain. *"But will God indeed dwell on the earth? behold, the heaven and heaven of heavens cannot contain thee; how much less this house that I have builded"* (1 Kings 8:27)? The human body of Jesus has ascended into heaven, *"why stand ye gazing up into heaven? this same Jesus, which is taken up from you into heaven, shall so come in like manner as ye have seen him go into heaven"* (Acts 1"11b), but as God He is everywhere at once. This is His people's comfort as they are journeying to the Promised Land, knowing that Jesus by His Spirit is guiding their steps. *"As thou hast sent me into the world, even so have I also sent them into the world"* (John 17:18). Jesus Christ as man is in heaven awaiting His body, (the Church) to be complete with Him there. *"Father, I will that they also, whom thou hast given me, be with me where I am; that they may behold my glory, which thou hast given me: for thou lovedst me before the foundation of the world"* (John 17:24).

The advantage of His people is the knowledge that Jesus, (Our Head) is in Heaven with our flesh as King of kings, so that there is nothing that will ever come between, separating us from His love. *"Even when we were dead in sins, hath quickened us together with Christ, (by grace ye are saved;) And hath raised us up together, and made us sit together in heavenly places in Christ Jesus: That in the ages to come he might show the exceeding riches of his grace in his kindness toward us through Christ Jesus:* (Ephesians 2:5-7). Does meditating on these things makes us long for their completion to lift us above the things of this present world, weaning us from the world? "*If ye then be risen with Christ, seek those things which are above, where Christ sitteth on the right hand of God. Set your affection on things above, not on things on the earth. For ye are dead, and your life is hid with Christ in God:* (Colossians 1-3). Does the world and everything in it still satisfy you? What things fill your heart and mind? "*Whose end is destruction, whose God is their belly, and whose glory is in their shame, who mind earthly things)*" (Philippians 3:19). Or! "*For our conversation is in heaven; from whence also we look for the Saviour, the Lord Jesus Christ: Who shall change our vile body, that it may be fashioned like unto his glorious body, according to the working whereby he is able even to subdue all things unto himself*" (Philippians 3:20-21).

26.
The God-Man King on the Throne

QUESTION: 50. WHY IS IT added, "and sitteth at the right hand of God"?

ANSWER: BECAUSE CHRIST IS ASCENDED into heaven for this end, that He might appear as head of His church, by whom the Father governs all things.

QUESTION: 51. WHAT PROFIT IS this glory of Christ our head, unto us?

ANSWER: FIRST, THAT BY HIS Holy Spirit He pours out heavenly graces upon us his members; and then by His power He defends and preserves us against all enemies.

The right hand is known as the place of honor and glory for conquerors. "*Which he* (God the Father) *wrought in Christ, when he raised him from the dead, and set him at his own right hand in the heavenly places, Far above all principality, and power, and might, and dominion, and every name that is named, not only in this world, but also in that which is to come: And hath put all things under his feet, and gave him to be the head over all things to the church, Which is his body, the fulness of him that filleth all in all."* (Ephesians 1:20-23). Christ loves His church so much, (which He proved by His Humiliation). He gave Himself for her, making her holy by the bloody righteousness He earned by His death, which was sealed in His resurrection, so as the ascended Lord, He defends and preserves her for Himself forever. *"My sheep hear my voice, and I know them, and they follow me: And I give unto them eternal life; and they shall never perish, neither shall any man pluck them out of my hand"* (John 10:27-28). The church on earth, (though often tossed and buffeted as the disciples experienced in the ship expecting any moment to sink away) learns His eye is always on them and all His people. They cannot perish because deliverance will come at His time bringing them safe into the harbor.

Praise the Lord for He is good, for His mercies ever sure
From eternity have stood, to eternity endure;
Let His ransomed people raise songs to their Redeemer's praise.

From captivity released, from the south and from the north,
From the west and from the east,
in His love He brought them forth,
Ransomed out of every land from the adversary's hand

Sons of men, awake to praise God the Lord Who reigns above,
Gracious in His works and ways, wondrous in redeeming love;
Longing souls He satisfies, hungry hearts with good supplies.
Psalter 292:1-2&5

27.
Christ as Judge the Comfort of His People

QUESTION: 52. WHAT COMFORT IS it to thee that "Christ shall come again to judge the quick and the dead"?

ANSWER: THAT IN ALL MY sorrows and persecutions, with uplifted head I look for the very same person, who before offered himself for my sake, to the tribunal of God, and has removed all curse from me, to come as judge from heaven: who shall cast all his and my enemies into everlasting condemnation, but shall translate me with all his chosen ones to himself, into heavenly joys and glory.

God's people are a poor and needy people in themselves. They need Jesus Christ to be their guide through this life conforming them more and more to His image. Though they have come short in every way, Jesus is their strength and refuge alone. *"For I will be merciful to their unrighteousness, and their sins and their iniquities will I remember no more"* (Hebrews 8:12). He, (Jesus) sees them as perfect because His blood has cleansed them from all sin. *"If we confess our sins, he is faithful and just to forgive us our sins, and to cleanse us from all unrighteousness"* (1 John 1:9). The Judge of all the earth is their Redeemer and Friend, who shall make them afraid? This is the One who said, *"Let not your heart be troubled: ye believe in God, believe also in me. In my Father's house are many mansions: if it were not so, I would have told you. I go to prepare a place for you. And if I go and prepare a place for you, I will come again, and receive you unto myself; that where I am, there ye may be also"* (John 14:1-3). Their comfort is in Him alone, who has loved them and promised never to leave or forsake them. This gives them the desire to be with Him where He is as our love for Him grows stronger. *"Henceforth there is laid up for me a crown of righteousness, which the Lord, the righteous judge, shall give me at that day: and not to me only, but unto all them also that love his appearing"* (2 Timothy 4:8). The Catechism asked at the beginning, "What is thy only comfort in life and death?" This asks us to look inward as to where our comfort is! The comfort of the world is temporary at best and shall end at death, but to know Him (Jesus Christ) as your Lord and King is never ending comfort.

In sweet communion, Lord with Thee I constantly abide;
My hand Thou holdest in Thy own to keep me near Thy side.
Thy counsel through my earthly way shall guide me and control,
And then to glory afterward Thou wilt receive my soul.
Whom have I, Lord, in heav'n but Thee, to whom my tho'ts aspire?
And having thee, on earth is nought that I can yet desire.
Tho' flesh and heart should faint and fail, the Lord will ever be
The strength and portion of my heart, my God eternally.
To live apart from God is death, 'tis good His face to seek;
My refuge is the living God, His praise I long to speak.
Psalter 203 taken from Psalm 73

28.
God the Holy Ghost

QUESTION: 53. WHAT DOST THOU believe concerning the Holy Ghost?

ANSWER: FIRST, THAT HE IS true and co-eternal God with the Father and the Son; secondly, that he is also given me, to make me by a true faith, partaker of Christ and all his benefits, that he may comfort me and abide with me forever.

The One true and eternal God is known as the Trinity, Father, Son, and Holy Ghost. The Holy Spirit is the one that is most active and yet the one that is least known. The Spirit takes the word as it goes out, opening hearts to understand the necessity of being reconciled with God. *"And when he,* (the Holy Spirit) *is come, he will reprove the world of sin, and of righteousness, and of judgment: Of sin, because they believe not on me; Of righteousness, because I go to my Father, and ye see me no more; Of judgment, because the prince of this world is judged"* (John 16:8-11). God, the Holy Ghost, is the one proceeding from the Father and the Son, making life to abound.

Jesus Christ, while on earth, told His disciples thet the Comforter would reveal things about Him they could not know any other way. *"Howbeit when he, the Spirit of truth, is come, he will guide you into all truth: for he shall not speak of himself; but whatsoever he shall hear, that shall he speak: and he will show you things to come. He shall glorify me: for he shall receive of mine, and shall show it unto you. All things that the Father hath are mine: therefore said I, that he shall take of mine, and shall show it unto you"* (John 16:13-15). Even more the Spirit dwells in His people. *"Know ye not that ye are the temple of God, and that the Spirit of God dwelleth in you"* (1 Corinthians 3:16).

O the love of God in Jesus Christ is a great comfort as we travel through enemy territory knowing that The Holy Spirit will give strength to endure whatever will befall us! *"And it is the Spirit that beareth witness, because the Spirit is truth"* (1 John 5:6b). The Holy Spirit seals this truth to our hearts. *"In whom ye also trusted, after that ye heard the word of truth, the gospel of your salvation: in whom also after that ye believed, ye were sealed with that holy Spirit of promise, Which is the earnest of our inheritance until the redemption of the purchased possession, unto the praise of his glory"* (Ephesians 1:13-14). We can at that moment sing praises to God because He has possessed our complete being, knowing we are His. *"And because ye are sons, God hath sent forth the Spirit of his Son into your hearts, crying, Abba, Father. Wherefore thou art no more a servant, but a son; and if a son, then an heir of God through Christ"* (Galatians 4:6-7).

Thy Spirit, O Lord, makes life to abound; the earth is renewed,
and fruitful the ground;
To God ascribe glory and wisdom and might, let God in His
creatures forever delight.

Rejoicing in God, my thought shall be sweet, while sinners
depart in ruin complete;
My soul bless Jehovah, His Name be adored, come, praise Him,
ye people, and worship the Lord.

Psalter 287:1and 3 taken from Psalm 104

29.
The Body of Christ

QUESTION: 54. WHAT BELIEVEST THOU concerning the "holy catholic church" of Christ?

ANSWER: THAT THE SON OF God from the beginning to the end of the world, gathers, defends, and preserves to himself by his Spirit and word, out of the whole human race a church chosen to everlasting life, agreeing in true faith; and that I am and for ever shall remain, a living member thereof.

QUESTION: 55. WHAT DO YOU understand by "the communion of saints"?

ANSWER: FIRST, THAT ALL AND every one, who believes, being members of Christ, are in common, partakers of him, and of all his riches and gifts; secondly, that every one must know it to be his duty, readily and cheerfully to employ his gifts, for the advantage and salvation of other members.

When speaking about the "holy catholic church." We mean a universal church gathered from every nation, tribe, and people sought out by Jesus Christ through His Word and Spirit into one body of believers, rescuing them from self-made spiritual death. *"I am come that they might have life, and that they might have it more abundantly"* (John 10:10b). He came and broke down the barriers which sin had erected, fulfilling all righteousness by His perfect life and atoning death on the cross. *"Elect according to the foreknowledge of God the Father, through sanctification of the Spirit, unto obedience and sprinkling of the blood of Jesus Christ: Grace unto you, and peace, be multiplied"* (1 Peter 1:2). The blood is all inclusive. It removes all sin, it is the shield of defense, and it is what preserves them from the wrath to come. *"Forasmuch as ye know that ye were not redeemed with corruptible things, as silver and gold, from your vain conversation received by tradition from your fathers; But with the precious blood of Christ, as of a lamb without blemish and without spot"* (1 Peter 1:18-19).

The love, which is so evident in the humiliation of Our Lord Jesus Christ, is the bond which binds His church together. *"We love him, because he first loved us"* (1 John 4:19). *"One Lord, one faith, one baptism, One God and Father of all, who is above all, and through all, and in you all"* (Ephesians 4:5-6). His people are one in Him, and all things are His so that His people are the recipients of them as His body. *"Therefore let no man glory in men. For all things are yours; Whether Paul, or Apollos, or Cephas, or the world, or life, or death, or things present, or things to come; all are yours; And ye are Christ's; and Christ is God's"* (1

Corinthians 3:21-23). This is the inheritance of God's people! Gold and silver is nothing compared to the glorious riches of Christ! It is in Him alone. Everything else is of no value.

30.
Forgiven

QUESTION: 56. WHAT BELIEVEST THOU concerning: the forgiveness of sins"?

ANSWER: THAT GOD, FOR THE sake of Christ's satisfaction, will no more remember my sins, neither, my corrupt nature, against which I have to struggle all my life long; but will graciously impute to me the righteousness of Christ, that I may never be condemned before the tribunal of God.

Sin brings separation, sleepless nights, and untold miseries! Sin brings fear or anger into our hearts, so that we would do most anything to be able to remain hidden from facing the one offended. This is seen already with our first parents, Adam and the Woman in the Garden of Eden after taking of the forbidden fruit. *"And they heard the voice of the LORD God walking in the garden in the cool of the day: and Adam and his wife hid themselves from the presence of the LORD God amongst the trees of the garden. And the LORD God called unto Adam, and said unto him, Where art thou? And he said, I heard thy voice in the garden, and I was afraid, because I was naked; and I hid myself"* (Genesis 3:8-10). This is being brought face to face with reality. Sin must be repented of. There must be reconciliation before there can be forgiveness! *"John did baptize in the wilderness, and preach the baptism of repentance for the remission of sins"* (Mark 1:4).

Repentance as hard as it is makes our heart pliable and receptive to asking for forgiveness! *"O God, according to thy lovingkindness: according unto the multitude of thy tender mercies blot out my transgressions. Wash me thoroughly from mine iniquity, and cleanse me from my sin. For I acknowledge my transgressions: and my sin is ever before me. Against thee, thee only, have I sinned, and done this evil in thy sight: that thou mightest be justified when thou speakest, and be clear when thou judgest"* (Psalm 51:1-4). Repentance unites the separated parties together. It brings peace and calmness in the place of anguish and pain as reconciliation is achieved. God brings His people face to face with Himself causing them to cry, "I am undone." This is a lifelong struggle because of our selfishness. Christ is the only remedy for reconciliation through His shed blood. At the cross forgiveness was made possible by His sacrifice. *"There is therefore now no condemnation to them which are in Christ Jesus, who walk not after the flesh, but after the Spirit"* (Romans 8:1). The forgiveness of God is so comprehensive. In spite our failures day by day against His love, it fills us with sorrow which is grounded in Jesus Christ. Jesus said through His prophet Isaiah, *"I have blotted out, as a thick cloud, thy transgressions, and, as a cloud, thy sins: return unto me; for I have redeemed thee"* (Isaiah 44:22). This is all our salvation now and forever. God in Christ gives repentance and faith through which we find the forgiveness of our sins. *"Him hath God exalted with his right hand to be a Prince and a Saviour, for to give repentance to Israel, and forgiveness of sins"* (Acts 5:31).

31.
The Resurrection and the Life

QUESTION: 57. WHAT COMFORT DOTH the "resurrection of the body" afford thee?

ANSWER: THAT NOT ONLY MY soul after this life shall be immediately taken up to Christ its head; but also, that this my body, being raised by the power of Christ, shall be reunited with my soul, and made like unto the glorious body of Christ.

QUESTION: 58. WHAT COMFORT TAKEST thou from the article of "life everlasting"?

ANSWER: THAT SINCE I NOW feel in my heart the beginning of eternal joy, after this life, I shall inherit perfect salvation, which "eye hath not seen, nor ear heard, neither hath it entered into the heart of man" to conceive, and that, to praise God therein for ever.

This is an amazing question! How can the thought of dying and the resurrection be a comfort? This question is asked by those who have no knowledge of who God is and what our end is without Him. They see God only as an austere judge, and not as their Savior King. *"But who may abide the day of his coming? and who shall stand when he appeareth? for he is like a refiner's fire, and like fullers' soap: And he shall sit as a refiner and purifier of silver: and he shall purify the sons of Levi, and purge them as gold and silver, that they may offer unto the LORD an offering in righteousness"* (Malachi 2:2-3).

God's people have been brought to see their sin. They also have found a place of repentance at the foot of the cross, hearing from His mouth, "Deliver *him from going down to the pit: I have found a ransom"* (Job 33:24b). This is a life changing event so that instead of despair there is hope! The grave becomes a vehicle to bring us into the presence of Christ, our head, and we experience more and more that the world is not our home. We begin to long for and pray to God when His love fills the soul, *"For to me to live is Christ, and to die is gain"* (Philippians 1:21). The comfort of the resurrection is that we will be with Him who has loved and saved us unto Himself. In the journey through the Catechism the reoccurring thought is, "What is thy only comfort?" This keeps us focused on Jesus Christ! *"Therefore we are always confident, knowing that, whilst we are at home in the body, we are absent from the Lord: (For we walk by faith, not by sight:) We are confident, I say, and willing rather to be absent from the body, and to be present with the Lord"* (2 Corinthians 5:6-8). To be away from home wearies us, but a view of Him who has taken our heart lifts our spirits in gratitude to Him.

My heart is fixed, O God, A grateful song I raise;
Awake, O harp, in joyful strains, awake, my soul, to praise.

Stretch forth Thy mighty hand in answer to our prayer,
And let Thy own beloved ones Thy great salvation share.

Psalter 299:1 and 4

32.
The Imputed Righteousness of Christ

QUESTION: 59. BUT WHAT DOTH it profit thee now that thou believest all this?

ANSWER: THAT I AM RIGHTEOUS in Christ, before God, and an heir of eternal life.

The question is a very personal question! It must become ours! Jesus Christ must become my righteousness! To believe that He is the Savior is a great blessing, but if it is not for me I am of all men most miserable. *"That I may know him, and the power of his resurrection, and the fellowship of his sufferings, being made conformable unto his death; If by any means I might attain unto the resurrection of the dead"* (Philippians 3:10-11).

The divine surgeon has shown us the corruption dwelling in us and with the knife of His Word has cut away the cancer in us (hatred of God, death) and implanted the healthy seed (faith, love to God, and eternal life). Now the things we loved before, we hate, and the things we hated before, we love. *"So when this* *corruptible shall have put on incorruption, and this mortal shall have put on immortality, then shall be brought to pass the saying that is written, Death is swallowed up in victory. O death, where is thy sting? O grave, where is thy victory? The sting of death is sin; and the strength of sin is the law. But thanks be to God, which giveth us the victory through our Lord Jesus Chri*st" (1 Corinthians 15:54-57). (Also Read Romans 7). The recovery faze has begun. This is a painful process, dying to self, being made alive in Christ. *"For therein is the righteousness of God revealed from faith to faith: as it is written, The just shall live by faith"* (Romans 1:17). Our eyes are opened to see Him, and our heart responds in adoration and worship being conformed to His likeness. The desire of our heart is to kill all remaining sin in us. We fail time and time again, but look unto Him for strength and endurance as the Lord's Supper form so beautifully says, "Therefore we rest assured that no sin or infirmity, which still remaineth against our will, in us, can hinder us from being received of God in mercy, and from being made worthy partakers of this heavenly meat and drink." In Him we have everything for time and eternity.

God is known among His people,
ev'ry mouth His praises fill;
From of old He hath established
His abode on Zion's hill;
There He broke the sword and arrow,
bade the noise of was be still.

Excellent and glorious art Thou,
with Thy trophies from the fray;
Thou hast slain the valiant hearted,
wrapt in sleep of death are they;
When Thy anger once is risen,
who can stand in that dread day?

When from heav'n Thy sentence sounded,
all the earth in fear was still,
While to save the meek and lowly
God in judgment wrought His will;
E'en the wrath of man shall praise Thee,
Thy designs it shall fulfill.

Vow and pay ye to Jehovah,
Him your God forever own;
All men bring your gifts before Him,
worship Him, and Him alone;
Mighty kings obey and fear Him,
princes bow before His throne.
Psalter 207, taken from Psalm 76

33.
Jesus Christ Our Righteousness

QUESTION: 60. How ART THOU righteous before God?

ANSWER: ONLY BY A TRUE faith in Jesus Christ; so that, though my conscience accuse me, that I have grossly transgressed all the commandments of God, and kept none of them, and am still inclined to all evil; notwithstanding, God, without any merit of mine, but only of grace, grants and imputes to me, the perfect satisfaction, righteousness and holiness of Christ; even so, as if I never had had, nor committed any sin: Christ has accomplished for me; inasmuch as I embrace such benefit with a believing heart.

QUESTION: 61. WHY SAYEST THOU, that thou art righteous by faith only?

ANSWER: NOT THAT I AM acceptable to God, on account of the worthiness of my faith; but because only the satisfaction, righteousness, and holiness of Christ, is my righteousness before

God; and that I cannot receive and apply the same to myself any other way than by faith only.

To be able to stand before God who is infinitely holy and righteous on our own account is impossible, but made possible in the righteousness of the Son of God. God becomes a necessity for me, but my sin stands in the way. God reveals to me, through the operation of the Holy Spirit, that missing Him is to miss the purpose of why we live. God's Word says, *"Believe on the Lord Jesus Christ and thou shalt be saved"* (Acts 16:31). We cry, *"Who is he, Lord, that I might believe on him"* (John 9:36b)? To hear Him say, *"Thou hast both seen him, and it is he that talketh with thee"* (John 9"37b). O! Then my heart is filled with love for Jesus Christ who worked this faith into my heart so that I may confess "My Lord and my God" (Luke 20:28b). Yes! This is my only comfort in life and death. *"For by grace are ye saved through faith; and that not of yourselves: it is the gift of God: Not of works, lest any man should boast"* (Ephesians 2:8-9). Who, out of His one-sided Sovereign grace, shed His blood as the God-man Savior, living a perfectly holy life every moment of every day earning for His people the righteousness they needed to be counted righteous before the Triune God. *"Yet it pleased the LORD to bruise him; he hath put him to grief: when thou shalt make his soul an offering for sin, he shall see his seed, he shall prolong his days, and the pleasure of the LORD shall prosper in his hand. He shall see of the travail of his soul, and shall be satisfied: by his knowledge shall my righteous servant justify many; for he shall bear their iniquities"* (Isaiah 53:10-11). O, the love of God for

His elect people, of whom I am one, will fill their hearts with rejoicing as they sing, "*Amen: Blessing, and glory, and wisdom, and thanksgiving, and honour, and power, and might, be unto our God for ever and ever. Amen*" (Revelation 7:12).

34.
Debtors to Divine Love

QUESTION: 62. BUT WHY CANNOT our good works be the whole, or part of our righteousness before God?

ANSWER: BECAUSE, THAT THE RIGHTEOUSNESS, which can be approved of before the tribunal of God, must be absolutely perfect, and in all respects conformable to the divine law; and also, that our best works in this life are all imperfect and defiled with sin.

QUESTION: 63. WHAT! DO NOT our good works merit, which yet God will reward in this and in a future life?

ANSWER: THIS REWARD IS NOT of merit, but of grace.

QUESTION: 64. BUT DOTH NOT this doctrine make men careless and profane?

ANSWER. BY NO MEANS: FOR it is impossible that those, who are implanted into Christ by a true faith, should not bring forth fruits of thankfulness.

Love for a special person brings a desire to do things that pleases them. As normal human beings we want to show our love so that that they would have deeper feelings for us. It is in many ways a selfish love. There is no righteousness in us, and God demands perfection! "*But we are all as an unclean thing, and all our righteousnesses are as filthy rags; and we all do fade as a leaf; and our iniquities, like the wind, have taken us away*" (Isaiah 64:6). We are such self lovers even after received grace and do works that make us look good until the Holy Spirit convicts us of our foolishness. Everything that we do must be to the glory and honor of God. "*For as many as are of the works of the law are under the curse: for it is written, Cursed is every one that continueth not in all things which are written in the book of the law to do them*" (Galatians 3:10). Sorrow fills our heart because we have sinned against the Lord Jesus Christ and His perfect love which He displayed in His perfect sacrifice on the cross for me. This excites in us a desire to please Him! This sends us to Him for strength. He said, "*I am the vine, ye are the branches: He that abideth in me, and I in him, the same bringeth forth much fruit: for without me ye can do nothing*" (John 15:5). Our hearts are filled with gratitude to the Lord for His life-giving blood. Instead of becoming careless and profane, His love humbles us so that our love for Him increases and we look around and see souls going lost needing His word brought to them. Eternity will be too short to repay back the love of God shown to us through Jesus Christ by the Holy Ghost. "*Herein is my Father glorified, that ye bear much fruit; so shall ye be my disciples*" (John 15:8).

Lord, speak to me,
that I may speak in living echoes of Thy tone;
As Thou hast sought,
so let me seek Thy erring children lost and lone.
O teach me, Lord,
that I may teach the precious things Thou dost impart;
And wing my words,
that they may reach the hidden depths of many a heart.
O fill me with Thy fullness, Lord,
until my very heart o'er flow
In kindling thought and glowing word
Thy love to tell, Thy praise to show.
O use me, Lord, use even me,
just as Thou wilt and when and where;
Until Thy blessed face I see,
Thy rest, Thy joy, Thy glory share. Amen.
Author Frances Ridley Havergal

35.
The Sacraments

QUESTION: 65. SINCE THEN WE are made partakers of Christ, and all his benefits by faith only, whence doth this faith proceed?

ANSWER: FROM THE HOLY GHOST, who works faith in our hearts by the preaching of the gospel, and confirms it by the use of the sacraments.

QUESTION: 66. WHAT ARE THE sacraments?

ANSWER: THE SACRAMENTS ARE HOLY visible signs and seals, appointed of God for this end, that by the use thereof, he may the more fully declare and seal to us the promise of the gospel, viz., that he grants us freely the remission of sin, and life eternal, for the sake of that one sacrifice of Christ, accomplished on the cross.

QUESTION: 67. ARE BOTH WORD and sacraments, then ordained and appointed for this end, that they may direct our faith to the sacrifice of Jesus Christ on the cross, as the only ground of our salvation?

ANSWER: YES, INDEED: FOR THE Holy Ghost teaches us in the gospel, and assures us by the sacraments, that the whole of our salvation depends upon that one sacrifice of Christ which he offered for us on the cross.

QUESTION: 68. HOW MANY SACRAMENTS has Christ instituted in the new covenant, or testament?

ANSWER: TWO: NAMELY HOLY BAPTISM, and the holy supper.

The Triune God, from all eternity, for reasons only known to Him, elected a church to salvation for His own glory and honor, so that they might glorify Him and enjoy Him forever. *"For by grace are ye saved through faith; and that not of yourselves: it is the gift of God"* (Ephesians 2:8). Though elected before the worlds were, they are called in time by the preaching of the gospel, (Word), worked in the heart by the Holy Ghost. As His church on earth travels to their eternal home, Christ has given signs and seals to confirm His promises to them. These are as an oasis in the wilderness for them, to remind them what their Lord Jesus Christ paid for their salvation with His precious blood, and strengthening them for the journey ahead by the sacraments. Through this, sin becomes exceedingly sinful to us, and strengthens our resolve to live our lives to His glory. *"What shall we say then? Shall we continue in sin, that grace may abound? God forbid. How shall we, that are dead to sin, live any longer therein"* (Romans 6:1-2)? The children of Israel had circumcision and the Passover, both bloody sacrifices as they looked forward to the one sacrifice of Christ on the cross, but now the fulness of time had come, the blood of the Redeemer had been shed. The sacraments, Baptism and the Lord's Supper, are bloodless showing that the sacrifice of Jesus Christ satisfied the justice of God forever.

Praise God, ye servants of the Lord, praise,
praise His Name with on accord;
Bless ye the Lord,
His Name adore from this time forth for evermore.
He lifts the poor and makes them great,
with joy He fills the desolate;
Praise ye the Lord and bless His Name,
His mercy and His might proclaim.
Psalter 306:1and 4. From Psalm 113

36.
God's Promises Strengthen by Holy Baptism

QUESTION: 69. How ART THOU admonished and assured by Holy Baptism, that the one sacrifice of Christ upon the cross is of real advantage to thee?

ANSWER: Thus: That Christ appointed this external washing with water adding thereto this promise, that I am as certainly washed by his blood and Spirit from all the pollution of my soul, that is, from all my sins as I am washed externally with water, by which the filthiness of the body is commonly washed away.

We wash our bodies to remove the accumulated dirt and clean up our appearance to be acceptable to those we met. This washing is done by each of us without the help of others. God sends His servants into the world with the commission, "*Go ye therefore, and teach all nations, baptizing them in the name of the Father, and of the Son, and of the Holy Ghost*" (Matthew 28:19). Baptism is the outward sign of the cleansing of the heart which we cannot do ourselves. It points to the one sacrifice of Christ on the cross. The Holy Spirit shows us the utter filthiness of our soul, humbling us before God, and seeking to be purified outside of ourselves, as the form for Administration of baptism says so richly. The Word goes out, "*He that believeth and is baptized shall be saved; but he that believeth not shall be damned*" (Mark 16:16).

Baptism is not salvation, but a sign and seal of God's covenant of grace with us. The promise is our pleading ground for our children and grandchildren. Baptism calls us to be separate from the world. "*Now the LORD had said unto Abram, Get thee out of thy country, and from thy kindred, and from thy father's house, unto a land that I will show thee: And I will establish my covenant between me and thee and thy seed after thee in their generations for an everlasting covenant, to be a God unto thee, and to thy seed after thee*" (Genesis 12:1 and 17:7). The Lord requires our whole heart. We cannot serve Him and the world at the same time. What do the promises of God mean to you?

O Lord of Hosts, how lovely Thy tabernacles are;
For them my heart is yearning in banishment afar.
My soul is longing fainting, Thy sacred courts to see;
My heart and flesh are crying, O living God, for Thee.

Beneath Thy care the sparrow finds place for peaceful rest;
To keep her young in safety the swallow finds a nest;
Then, Lord, my King Almighty, Thy love will shelter me;
Beside Thy holy altar my dwelling place shall be.

Blest they who dwell in Zion, whose joy and strength Thou art;
Forever they will praise Thee, Thy ways are in their heart.
Tho' tried, their tears like showers shall fill the springs of peace,
And all the way to Zion their strength shall still increase.
Psalter 227 taken from Psalm 84

37.
Baptism Signifies Remission of Our Sins

QUESTION: 70. WHAT IS IT to be washed with the blood and Spirit of Christ?

ANSWER: IT IS TO RECEIVE of God the remission of sins, freely, for the sake of Christ's blood, which he shed for us by his sacrifice upon the cross; and also to be renewed by the Holy Ghost, and sanctified to be members of Christ, that as we may more and more die unto sin, and lead holy and unblameable lives.

QUESTION: 71. WHERE HAS CHRIST promised us, that he will as certainly wash us by his blood and Spirit, as we are washed with the water of baptism?

ANSWER: IN THE INSTITUTION OF baptism which is thus expressed: "Go ye therefore, and teach all nations, baptizing them in the name of the Father, and of the Son, and of the Holy Ghost: and He that believeth and is baptized shall be saved;

but he that believeth not shall be damned." This promise is also repeated, where the scripture calls baptism the washing of regeneration, and the washing away of sins.

Baptism is the visible sign of the washing away of sins by the blood of Jesus Christ. Jesus Christ, who is the propitiation for the sins of His people, becomes exceedingly precious as our righteousness! He is the Fountain for cleansing, the Word of life, and the Shepherd to lead us! Jesus Christ is everything for sinners who have come to see their utter dependence on Him. They can only stand because of His bloody righteousness which He freely gives to them. *"Being justified freely by his grace through the redemption that is in Christ Jesus: Whom God hath set forth to be a propitiation through faith in his blood, to declare his righteousness for the remission of sins that are past, through the forbearance of God; To declare, I say, at this time his righteousness: that he might be just, and the justifier of him which believeth in Jesus"* (Romans 3:24-26). Also *"And I give unto them eternal life; and they shall never perish, neither shall any man pluck them out of my hand"* (John 10:28). It is a cleansing that brings a dying to self and making alive in Christ. *"Therefore we are buried with him by baptism into death: that like as Christ was raised up from the dead by the glory of the Father, even so we also should walk in newness of life"* (Romans 6:4).

This opens the mouth of the redeemed to go tell what wonderous things God has done for them. As they go forth the Holy Ghost opens hearts to not only receive the word but also respond to it. *"And now why tarriest thou? arise, and be baptized, and wash away thy sins, calling on the name of the Lord"* (Acts

22:16). Baptism is not salvation, it is a visible display of God being gracious and merciful to all those who believe His word 'that there is forgiveness with Him that He might be feared' See Psalm 130.4). *"Not by works of righteousness which we have done, but according to his mercy he saved us, by the washing of regeneration, and renewing of the Holy Ghost; Which he shed on us abundantly through Jesus Christ our Saviour; That being justified by his grace, we should be made heirs according to the hope of eternal life"* (Titus 3:5).

38.
What Can Wash away My Sin?

QUESTION: 72. IS THEN THE external baptism with water the washing away of sin itself?

ANSWER: NOT AT ALL: FOR the blood of Jesus Christ only, and the Holy Ghost cleanse us from all sin.

QUESTION: 73. WHY THEN DOTH the Holy Ghost call baptism "the washing of regeneration," and "the washing away of sin?

ANSWER: GOD SPEAKS THUS NOT without great cause, to-wit, not only thereby to teach us, that as the filth of the body is purged away by water, so our sins are removed by the blood and Spirit of Jesus Christ; but especially that by this divine pledge and sign he may assure us, that we are spiritually cleansed from our sins as really, as we are externally washed with water.

John the Baptist, when asked who he was, answered that he was only a voice, proclaiming the way of the Lord, calling for repentance of sin. He baptized those that did so, but also said to those who questioned him, "*I indeed have baptized you with water: but he shall baptize you with the Holy Ghost*" (Mark 1:8). John pointed the people that came to him away from himself to Jesus as the true Cleanser from sin. "*The next day John seeth Jesus coming unto him, and saith, Behold the Lamb of God, which taketh away the sin of the world*" (John 1:29). Yes! The external water cannot cleanse or remove the stain of sin, but "*the blood of Jesus Christ cleanseth us from all sin*" (1 John 1:7b). Salvation is the work of the Triune God. The Father gave His Son to work salvation. God the Son purchased salvation with His suffering and death on the cross, and God the Holy Ghost by the Word prepares hearts for the cleansing power of the blood. The Holy Ghost reveals Jesus Christ and His righteousness as the only one who is able to cleanse or wash us from the infinite stain of sin. "*And from Jesus Christ, who is the faithful witness, and the first begotten of the dead, and the prince of the kings of the earth. Unto him that loved us, and washed us from our sins in his own blood, And hath made us kings and priests unto God and his Father; to him be glory and dominion for ever and ever. Amen*" (Revelation 1:5-6). The blood of Jesus Christ is the only antidote for acceptance before God. This is the "New Birth" the washing of regeneration, the baptism with the Holy Ghost. Nothing less will do, and more is not needed!

> Lord, my hope is in Thy promise, and I wait for Thee
> More then they who watch for morning, light to see.

With the Lord is tender mercy, and redeeming love,
Israel, look for full salvation from above
Psalter 365:3 and 4 taken from Psalm 130

39.
God's Covenant Revealed

QUESTION: 74. ARE INFANTS ALSO to be baptized?

ANSWER: YES: FOR SINCE THEY, as well as the adult, are included in the covenant and church of God; and since redemption from sin by the blood of Christ, and the Holy Ghost, the author of faith, is promised to them no less than to the adult; they must therefore by baptism, as a sign of the covenant, be also admitted into the Christian church; and be distinguished from the children of unbelievers as was done in the old covenant or testament by circumcision, instead of which baptism is instituted in the new covenant.

God came to Adam and Eve in the garden after they fell, revealing to them though they deserved eternal death, that He had prepared from eternity past a remedy, taking reason out of Himself to save a remnant unto Himself. "*And I will put enmity between thee and the woman, and between thy seed and her seed; it shall bruise thy head, and thou shalt bruise his heel*"

(Genesis 3:15). In this revelation God shows that there would be two families, Satan's and the Lord's. God's seed would be saved or redeemed by blood, (the covenant of grace). "*And I will establish my covenant between me and thee and thy seed after thee in their generations for an everlasting covenant, to be a God unto thee, and to thy seed after thee*" (Genesis 17:7). This is the wonder of Sovereign Grace as God gathers a church to praise and worship Him. "*Gather the people, sanctify the congregation, assemble the elders, gather the children, and those that suck the breasts: let the bridegroom go forth of his chamber, and the bride out of her closet*" (Joel 2:16). God loves His church so that Satan cannot hinder its advancement. "*Instead of thy fathers shall be thy children, whom thou mayest make princes in all the earth. I will make thy name to be remembered in all generations: therefore shall the people praise thee for ever and ever*" (Psalm 45:16-17).

God commanded Israel to circumcise all the male children in the old covenant setting them apart from this world as His children. After the one sacrifice of Christ, baptism was put in its place. "*While Peter yet spake these words, the Holy Ghost fell on all them which heard the word. Can any man forbid water, that these should not be baptized, which have received the Holy Ghost as well as we*" (Acts 10:44 and 47)? O! The mercy of God is displayed in the continuance of His church through all ages to His glory. One day a number of both young and old that no man can count shall praise Him forever! Baptism does not save, but Jesus Christ does. He said, "*Suffer the little children to come unto me, and forbid them not: for of such is the kingdom of God. Verily I say unto you, Whosoever shall not receive the kingdom of*

God as a little child, he shall not enter therein" (Mark 10:14b-15). Have you been baptized or washed in His blood by the Holy Spirit?

40.
God's Promises Strengthened by His Holy Supper

QUESTION: 75. How ART THOU admonished and assured in the Lord's Supper, that thou art a partaker of that one sacrifice of Christ, accomplished on the cross, and of all his benefits?

ANSWER: THUS: THAT CHRIST HAS commanded me and all believers, to eat of this broken bread, and to drink of this cup, in remembrance of him, adding these promises: first, that his body was offered and broken on the cross for me, and his blood shed for me, as certainly as I see with my eyes, the bread of the Lord broken for me, and the cup communicated to me; and further, that he feeds and nourishes my soul to everlasting life, with his crucified body and shed blood, as assuredly as I receive from the hands of the minister, and taste with my mouth the bread and cup of the Lord, as certain signs of the body and blood of Christ.

QUESTION: 76. WHAT IS IT then to eat the crucified body, and drink the shed blood of Christ?

ANSWER: It is not only to embrace with a believing heart all the sufferings and death of Christ, and thereby to obtain the pardon of sin, and life eternal; but also, besides that, to become more and more united to his sacred body, by the Holy Ghost, who dwells both in Christ and in us; so that we, though Christ is in heaven and we on earth, are notwithstanding "Flesh of his flesh, and bone of his bone"; and that we live, and are governed forever by one spirit, as members of the same body are by one soul.

When Christ instituted the Lord's Supper on the night before His sacrifice of Himself on the cross, He said to His disciples, "*With desire I have desired to eat this passover with you before I suffer*" (Luke 22:15b). What a display of how Our Lord Jesus Christ loves His people with complete disregard of His physical suffering and pain! "*Now before the feast of the passover, when Jesus knew that his hour was come that he should depart out of this world unto the Father, having loved his own which were in the world, he loved them unto the end*" (John 13:1). This love brings out the love of God in the hearts of His people, so that they cannot but love Him in return! Jesus, Himself, is the host and He breaks the bread saying, "*Take, eat: this is my body*" (Mark 14:22b), and takes the cup, gave thanks and said, "saying, *Drink ye all of it; For this is my blood of the new testament, which is shed for many for the remission of sins*" (Matthew 26:27b-28). He did all this only for His church so that they would not forget Him as, "*the author and finisher of our faith*" (Hebrews 12:2b). His people are strengthened as they see the promises fulfilled in Him alone. They receive momentary joy, but also a desire to have that joy fulfilled by His promise to come again and take them unto Himself. "*But I say unto you, I will not drink henceforth of this fruit of the vine, until that day when I drink it new with you in my Father's kingdom*" Matthew 26:29). We may stumble and fall, but He says, "*Fear thou not; for I am with thee: be not dismayed; for I am thy God: I will strengthen thee; yea, I will help thee; yea, I will uphold thee with the right hand of my righteousness*" (Isaiah 41:10). It is Jesus Christ alone. Without His upholding power, we and all His people would fail, but He is always making intersession for us. "*Wherefore he is able also to save them to the uttermost that come unto God by him, seeing he ever liveth to make intercession for them*" (Hebrews 7:25). Is this Jesus your only comfort here in this life? If so He shall be your comfort forever and ever!

41.
Christ the Fulfillment of the Promises

QUESTION: 77. WHERE HAS CHRIST promised that he will as certainly feed and nourish believers with his body and blood, as they eat of this broken bread, and drink of this cup?

ANSWER: IN THE INSTITUTION OF the supper, which is thus expressed: "The Lord Jesus, the same night in which he was betrayed, took bread, and when he had given thanks, he brake it, and said: eat, this is my body, which is broken for you; this do in remembrance of me. After the same manner also he took the cup, when had supped, saying: this cup is the new testament in my blood; this do ye, as often as ye drink it, in remembrance of me. For, as often as ye eat this bread, and drink this cup, ye do show the Lord's death till he come."

This promise is repeated by the holy apostle Paul, where he says: "The cup of blessing which we bless, is it not the communion of the blood of Christ? The bread which we break, is it not the communion of the body of Christ? For we, being many are one bread and one body; because we are all partakers of that one bread."

As the Lord's Supper is celebrated in the church, it is the visible gospel of the faithfulness of the Triune God. As Father He wrought salvation for His elect, as Son He bought salvation for His elect, as Holy Ghost He applies salvation for His elect. *"Then Jesus said unto them, Verily, verily, I say unto you, Moses gave you not that bread from heaven; but my Father giveth you the true bread from heaven. For the bread of God is he which cometh down from heaven, and giveth life unto the world. I am the bread of life: he that cometh to me shall never hunger; and he that believeth on me shall never thirst"* (John 6:32-33 and 35).

The world sees no worthiness in Jesus Christ and despises Him. His people not only see His worthiness, but have learned that to live without Him is death. *"Unto you therefore which believe he is precious: but unto them which be disobedient, the stone which the builders disallowed, the same is made the head of the corner, And a stone of stumbling, and a rock of offence, even to them which stumble at the word, being disobedient: whereunto also they were appointed"* (1 Peter 2:7-8). This is what the Divine Surgeon has been working, renewing us not only for a holy life here on earth, but to be made perfect to dwell with Him forever. There we shall feast on Him forever in that never ending day of glory. All praise, honor, and worship shall be to this God, Father, Son, and Holy Ghost as we feed in green pastures, beside the river of God. *"And he showed me a pure river of water of life, clear as crystal, proceeding out of the throne of God and of the Lamb. In the midst of the street of it, and on either side of the river, was there the tree of life, which bare twelve manner of fruits, and yielded her fruit every month: and the leaves of the tree were for the healing of the nations. And there shall be no more curse: but the throne of God and of the Lamb shall be in it; and his servants shall serve him: And they shall see his face; and his name shall be in their foreheads. And there shall be no night there; and they need no candle, neither light of the sun; for the Lord God giveth them light: and they shall reign for ever and ever"* (Revelation 22:1-5).

42.
Temporal Means a Spiritual Pledge

QUESTION: 78. Do THEN THE bread and wine become the very body and blood of Christ?

ANSWER: NOT AT ALL: BUT as the water in baptism is not changed into the blood of Christ, neither is the washing away of sin itself, being only the sign and confirmation thereof appointed of God; so the bread in the Lord's supper is not changed into the very body of Christ; though agreeably to the nature and properties of sacraments, it is called the body of Jesus Christ.

QUESTION: 79. WHY THEN DOTH Christ call the bread his body and the cup his blood, or the new covenant in his blood; and Paul the "communion of the body and blood of Christ?

ANSWER: CHRIST SPEAKS THUS, NOT without great reason, namely not only thereby to teach us, that as bread and wine support this temporal life, so his crucified body and shed blood are the true meat and drink, whereby our souls are fed to eternal life; but more especially by these visible signs and pledges to assure us, that we are as really partakers of his true body and blood (by the operation of the Holy Ghost) as we receive by the mouths of our bodies these holy signs in remembrance of him; and that all his sufferings and obedience are certainly ours, as if we had in our own persons suffered and made satisfaction for our sins.

God, (in His Word) uses signs and seals to help us to understand a little of the deep mysteries of who He is. We are so ignorant of God and His ways, and need guidance in our travel through this wilderness. *"Moreover, brethren, I would not that ye should be ignorant, how that all our fathers were under the cloud, and all passed through the sea; And were all baptized unto Moses in the cloud and in the sea; And did all eat the same spiritual meat; And did all drink the same spiritual drink: for they drank of that spiritual Rock that followed them: and that Rock was Christ"* (1 Corinthians 10:1-4). When the sacraments are being used with the elements as if they could save us, they cannot but must point to the Rock, Jesus Christ! *"And Jesus said unto them, I am the bread of life: he that cometh to me shall never hunger; and he that believeth on me shall never thirst"* (John 6:35). Nothing else will do! It is a spiritual hunger and thirst after the righteousness of Jesus Christ. *"As the hart panteth after the water brooks, so panteth my soul after thee, O God. My soul thirsteth for God, for the living God: when shall I come and appear before God"* (Psalm 42:1-2). As we partake of the bread and the wine our hunger and thirst is temporally quenched, and at the same time we are longing for the eternal fulfillment which is Christ. *"Therefore are they before the throne of God, and serve him day and night in his temple: and he that sitteth on the throne shall dwell among them. They shall hunger no more, neither thirst any more; neither shall the sun light on them, nor any heat. For the Lamb which is in the midst of the throne shall feed them, and shall lead them unto living fountains of waters: and God shall wipe away all tears from their eyes"* (Revelation 7:15-17). The temporal means point to the eternal Satisfier!

43.
God's Word or Man's Word

QUESTION: 80. WHAT DIFFERENCE IS there between the Lord's supper and the popish mass?

ANSWER: THE LORD'S SUPPER TESTIFIES to us, that we have a full pardon of all sin by the only sacrifice of Jesus Christ, which he, himself has once accomplished on the cross; and, that we by the Holy Ghost are ingrafted into Christ, who, according to his human nature is now not on earth, but in heaven, at the right hand of God his Father, and will there be worshipped by us: --but the mass teaches, that the living and dead have not the pardon of sins through the sufferings of Christ, unless that Christ is also daily offered for them by the priests; and further, that Christ is bodily under the form of bread and wine, and therefore is to be worshipped in them; so that the mass, at bottom is nothing else than a denial of the one sacrifice and sufferings of Jesus Christ, and an accursed idolatry.

Since the fall of man in Paradise, and his expulsion from the Garden, man has tried many ways to find a way back into the good graces of their Creator God. *"Lo, this only have I found, that God hath made man upright; but they have sought out many inventions"* (Ecclesiastes 7:29). What seemingly pious way Satan uses through the religious element of the church. This is just tailor made for our corrupt hearts. Israel in the wilderness wanted a god they could see and worship, making the golden calf. (Read Exodus 32). *"He that speaketh of himself seeketh his own glory: but he that seeketh his glory that sent him, the same is true, and no unrighteousness is in him"* (John 7:18). Man wants to be a god unto himself.

But God, who knows the heart of man, opens the heart and exposes our wickedness bringing us to despair with all our man-made idols. So man's word becomes worthless, yes even dangerous, and His Word our only hope. God accomplishes this as He strips away every one of our own righteousnesses, leaving us naked, and needing His righteousness outside of ourselves. This gives God's Word the preeminence, driving us to the Word, *"Scriptures which are able to make us wise unto salvation"* (2 Timothy 3:15b). We are brought to the cross of Christ for our justification. *"And you, being dead in your sins and the uncircumcision of your flesh, hath he quickened together with him, having forgiven you all trespasses; Blotting out the handwriting of ordinances that was against us, which was contrary to us, and took it out of the way, nailing it to his cross; And having spoiled principalities and powers, he made a show of them openly, triumphing over them in it"* (Colossians 2:13-15). The popish mass is what dwells in our hearts by nature and is an accursed idolatry, "*Whose end is destruction, whose God is their belly, and whose glory is in their shame, who mind earthly things)*" (Philippians 3:19). Have you learned that salvation, is not the work of man, or the work of God and man, but rests only in God alone through Jesus blood and righteousness?

Thy burden now cast on the Lord,
and He shall thy weakness sustain;
The righteous who trust in His word
unmoved shall forever remain.
Psalter 150:4

44.
The Lord's Supper for Saved Sinners

QUESTION: 81. FOR WHOM IS the Lord's supper instituted?

ANSWER: FOR THOSE WHO ARE truly sorrowful for their sins, and yet trust that these are forgiven them for the sake of Christ; and that their remaining infirmities are covered by his passion and death; and who also earnestly desire to have their faith more and more strengthened, and their lives more holy; but hypocrites, and such as turn not to God with sincere hearts, eat and drink judgment to themselves.

QUESTION: 82. ARE THEY ALSO to be admitted to this supper, who by confession, and life, declare themselves unbelieving and ungodly?

ANSWER: No; FOR BY THIS the covenant of God would be profaned and his wrath kindled against the whole congregation; therefore it is the duty of the Christian church, according to the appointment of Christ and his apostles, to exclude such persons, by the keys of the kingdom of heaven, till they show amendment of life.

To answer the question, who are fit participants for the Lord's Supper? The answer is none! *"As it is written, There is none righteous, no, not one: There is none that understandeth, there is none that seeketh after God"* (Romans 3:10-11). The righteousness needed is not to be found in us, but in Jesus Christ, the Savior of sinners. Sin must become sin; and the burden for this sin must drive us to Him in repentance for them. *"Now I rejoice, not that ye were made sorry, but that ye sorrowed to repentance: for ye were made sorry after a godly manner, that ye might receive damage by us in nothing. For godly sorrow worketh repentance to salvation not to be repented of: but the sorrow of the world worketh death"* (2 Corinthians 7:9-10). God who gives repentance also gives faith to believe so that they find forgiveness in the crucified Christ, and in Him they are made fit participants for the Holy Supper. It is impossible to please God without this confession. God in Jesus Christ makes unworthy partakers, worthy partakers! They do it in remembrance of Christ alone; any other ground is eating and drinking damnation to ourselves. *"Therefore thus saith the Lord GOD; Behold, mine anger and my fury shall be poured out upon this place, upon man, and upon beast, and upon the trees of the field, and upon the fruit of the ground; and it shall burn, and shall not be quenched"* (Jeremiah 7:20). The table must be fenced about to keep them from profaning it, but not so that God's poor and needy people are not kept away. The Table of the Lord is for sinners saved by grace, unworthy in self, but made worthy by the blood of Christ.

To Thee, O Lord, I lift my eye,
O Thou enthroned above the skies;
As servants watch their master's hand,
or maidens by their mistress stand,
So to the Lord our eyes we raise,
until His mercy He displays.
Psalm 351:1

45.
The Keys of the Kingdom

QUESTION: 83. WHAT ARE THE keys of the kingdom of heaven?

ANSWER: THE PREACHING OF THE holy gospel, and Christian discipline, or excommunication out of the Christian church; by these two, the kingdom of heaven is opened to believers, and shut to unbelievers.

QUESTION: 84. How IS THE kingdom of heaven opened and shut by the preaching of the holy gospel?

ANSWER: THUS: WHEN ACCORDING TO the command of Christ, it is declared and publicly testified to all and every believer, that whenever they receive the promise of the gospel by a true faith, all their sins are forgiven them of God, for the sake of Christ's merits; and on the contrary, when it is declared and testified to all unbelievers, and such as do not sincerely repent, that they stand exposed to the wrath of God, and eternal condemnation, so long as they are unconverted: according to this, and in the life to come.

QUESTION: 85. How is the kingdom of heaven shut and opened by Christian discipline?

ANSWER: Thus: when according to the command of Christ, those, who under the name of Christians, maintain doctrines, or practices inconsistent therewith, and will not, after having been often brotherly admonished, renounce their errors and wicked course of life, are complained of to the church, or to those who are thereunto appointed by the church; and if they despise their admonition, are by them forbidden the use of the sacraments; whereby they are excluded from the Christian church, and by God himself from the kingdom of Christ; and when they promise and show real amendment, are again received as members of Christ and his church.

The marks of the true church are the pure preaching of the word and Christian discipline. The church on earth is made up of sinners, "*For all have sinned, and come short of the glory of God*" (Romans 3:23). Jesus Christ came to earth to save sinners, "*For the promise is unto you, and to your children, and to all that are afar off, even as many as the Lord our God shall call*" (Acts 2:39). As the Word goes out through God's servants, the Holy Ghost accompanies the Word, opening hearts to believe the gospel to the saving of their soul. This opens the kingdom of heaven, "*And the Lord added to the church daily such as should be saved*" (Acts 2:47b). The preaching shuts out those that hear the word but do not repent. "*And when he (Jesus) had said this, he breathed on them, and saith unto them, Receive ye the Holy Ghost: Whose soever sins ye remit, they are remitted unto them; and whose soever sins ye retain, they are retained"* (John 20:22-23).

Discipline must be exercised when those who profess to believe fall into sin or teach false doctrine. The church of God must be kept pure of errors, which because of our sinful natures, will creep in if not dealt with. God give ministers and elders, who are watchmen on the walls, for this purpose. *"Let the elders that rule well be counted worthy of double honour, especially they who labour in the word and doctrine"* (1 Timothy 5:17). Discipline works to the glory of God and the unity of the church in Christ. Sin must be purged out. *"Them that sin rebuke before all, that others also may fear. Some men's sins are open beforehand, going before to judgment; and some men they follow after. If any man teach otherwise, and consent not to wholesome words, even the words of our Lord Jesus Christ, and to the doctrine which is according to godliness; He is proud, knowing nothing, but doting about questions and strifes of words, whereof cometh envy, strife, railings, evil surmisings, Perverse disputings of men of corrupt minds, and destitute of the truth, supposing that gain is godliness: from such withdraw thyself"* (1 timothy 5:20 24, and 6:4-5). This is shown in the letter to the church of Thyatira, *"And I gave her space to repent of her fornication; and she repented not. Behold, I will cast her into a bed, and them that commit adultery with her into great tribulation, except they repent of their deeds. And I will kill her children with death; and all the churches shall know that I am he which searcheth the reins and hearts: and I will give unto every one of you according to your works. But unto you I say, and unto the rest in Thyatira, as many as have not this doctrine, and which have not known the depths of Satan, as they speak; I will put upon you none other burden. But that which ye have already hold fast till I come"* (Revelation 2:21-25). Church discipline is to bring those who stray from the truth to see their error and repent and return. Love is always the motivation in disciplining. Those who repent are received again into the church and the kingdom of heaven is opened to them, but for the unrepentant it is shut. God is a God of order and will in no wise clear the guilty.

46.
Thankfulness Shown by Good Works

QUESTION: 86. SINCE THEN WE are delivered from our misery, merely of grace, through Christ, without any merit of ours, why must we still do good works?

ANSWER: BECAUSE CHRIST, HAVING REDEEMED and delivered us by his blood; also renews us by his Holy Spirit, after his own image; that we may testify, by the whole of our conduct, our gratitude to God for his blessings, and that he may be praised by us; also that every one may be assured in himself of his faith, by the fruits thereof; and that, by our godly conversation, others may be gained to Christ.

QUESTION: 87. CANNOT THEY THEN be saved, who, continuing in their wicked and ungrateful lives, are not converted to God?

ANSWER: BY NO MEANS; FOR the Holy scripture declares that no unchaste person, idolater, adulterer, thief, covetous man, drunkard, slanderer, robber, or any such like, shall inherit the kingdom of God.

A person, who is saved from drowning, will tell those around them about their savior out of gratitude. In a much greater sense, a sinner dead in sins and trespasses, is given eternal life out of mere sovereign grace for Jesus sake, who died to set him free. As Jesus told one He had healed, "*Go home to thy friends, and tell them how great things the Lord hath done for thee, and hath had compassion on thee*: (Mark 5:19b). This is gratitude indeed, but also fulfills the mandate of the Lord Jesus Christ as He ascended into heaven, "*Go ye therefore, and teach all nations, baptizing them in the name of the Father, and of the Son, and of the Holy Ghost: Teaching them to observe all things whatsoever I have commanded you: and, lo, I am with you alway, even unto the end of the world*" (Matthew 28:19-20). As the Word goes out, the Spirit opens hearts to receive it, "*and they are they which testify of me*" (John 6:39b). It is the love of God which motivates good works. Without this love, all our works are self centered and cannot be accepted by God. "*We know that we have passed from death unto life, because we love the brethren. He that loveth not his brother abideth in death. Whosoever hateth his brother is a murderer: and ye know that no murderer hath eternal life abiding in him*" (1 John 3:14-15). This eliminates any possibility of salvation outside of the life-giving blood of our Lord Jesus Christ. "*Ye must be born again*" (John 3:7b).

Salvation's joyful song is heard wher-e'er the righteous dwell;
For them God's hand is strong to save and doeth all things well.
I shall not die, but live and tell the wonders of the Lord;
He hath not giv'n my soul to death, but chastened and restored.
Psalter 317:4 Taken from Psalm 118

47.
True Conversion

QUESTION: 88. OF HOW MANY parts doth the true conversion of man consist?

ANSWER: OF TWO PARTS; OF the mortification of the old, and the quickening of the new man.

QUESTION: 89. WHAT IS THE mortification of the old man?

ANSWER: IT IS A SINCERE sorrow of heart, that we have provoked God by our sins; and more and more to hate and flee from them.

What does the word <u>conversion</u> mean? Interestingly the dictionary says, "A change from one belief, religion, doctrine, opinion, to another." It is more than just a change of belief, although it is that, it is a resurrection from the dead! "*And you hath he quickened, who were dead in trespasses and sins: Wherein in time past ye walked according to the course of this world, according to the prince of the power of the air, the spirit that now worketh in the children of disobedience: Among whom also we all had our conversation in times past in the lusts of our flesh, fulfilling the desires of the flesh and of the mind; and were by nature the children of wrath, even as others"* (Ephesians 2:1-3). This making alive gives us new desires. It changes our whole outlook of who we are and what we should be. God becomes real, His commandments become real, my failures become real, and I realize for the first time my need to be reconciled to this God! *"Wherefore he saith, Awake thou that sleepest, and arise from the dead, and Christ shall give thee light"* (Ephesians 5:14). I hate the things that I loved before, and love the things that I hated. O, the sorrow that fills our heart for our wickedness of sinning against such a longsuffering God. Sin becomes sin in our lives. I become the problem, and God, who is angry with the wicked, becomes my only option. God is drawing us to Himself, through our impossibilities, by His word to own our guilt. *"For I acknowledge my transgressions: and my sin is ever before me. Against thee, thee only, have I sinned, and done this evil in thy sight: that thou mightest be justified when thou speakest, and be clear when thou judgest"* (Psalm 51:3-4). We cannot go on in the way we were traveling, so that despite all odds, we will go to Him for to live without God is death, but a hope arises in our soul, *"I will arise and go to my father, and will say unto him, Father, I have sinned against heaven, and before thee, And am no more worthy to be called thy son: make me as one of thy hired servants"* (Luke 15:18-19). Even if it means death, I cannot continue to provoke God and so I flee to Him as my only hope! This is mortification of the old man. *"For by grace are ye saved through faith; and that not of yourselves: it is the gift of God: Not of works, lest any man should boast. For we are his workmanship, created in Christ Jesus unto good works, which God hath before ordained that we should walk in them"* (Ephesians 2:8-10). As it is the work of the Triune God, He will also quicken the new man.

48.
True Conversion Experienced

QUESTION: 90. WHAT IS THE quickening of the old man?

ANSWER: IT IS A SINCERE joy of heart in God, through Christ, and with love and delight to live according to the will of God in all good works.

QUESTION: 91. BUT WHAT ARE good works?

ANSWER: ONLY THOSE WHICH PROCEED from a true faith, are performed accordingly to the law of God, and to his glory; and not such as are founded on our imaginations, or the institutions of man.

When the Holy Spirit quickens a dead soul, He works a need in the soul for God! The joy he thought he had before becomes a reason for sorrow because sin was its object. Now God becomes the object of his desire to be living holily for Him only. "*For in that he died, he died unto sin once: but in that he liveth, he liveth unto God. Likewise reckon ye also yourselves to be dead indeed unto sin, but alive unto God through Jesus Christ our Lord. Let not sin therefore reign in your mortal body, that ye should obey it in the lusts thereof*" (Romans 6:10-12). He finds happiness and delight in walking in God's commandments. "*The statutes of the LORD are right, rejoicing the heart: the commandment of the LORD is pure, enlightening the eyes*" (Psalm 19:8). Although he falls short many times his heart's desire is to keep His law. "*O how love I thy law! it is my meditation all the day*" (Psalm 119:97). This dependence on God and His Word leads to good works. The Holy Spirit works faith in the heart to see both our sin and the preciousness of Christ, who kept the law perfectly for law breakers. Jesus Christ made us (His people) perfect in Himself through His blood and righteousness. "*The eyes of your understanding being enlightened; that ye may know what is the hope of his calling, and what the riches of the glory of his inheritance in the saints, And what is the exceeding greatness of his power to us-ward who believe, according to the working of his mighty power*" (Ephesians 1:18-19). This is the quickening of the new man. Man becomes nothing, and God, in Jesus Christ, becomes everything making all that we do for God's glory.

In thee, O Lord, I put my trust; shamed let me never be;
O save me in Thy righteousness, give ear and rescue me.

Be Thou my rock, my dwelling place, forever mine as now;
Salvation Thou hast willed for me, my rock and fortress Thou.

Deliver me from wicked hands, save me from men unjust,
For Thou, Jehovah, art my hope, from youth Thou art my trust.

Thou hast upheld me in Thy grace from child-hood's early days;
To Thee from Whom I life received will I give constant praise.
Psalter 190 Taken from Psalm 71

49.
God's Law of Love

QUESTION: 92. WHAT IS THE law of God?

ANSWER: GOD SPAKE ALL THESE words, Exodus 20, Deut.5, saying: I am the Lord thy God, which hath brought thee out of the land of Egypt, out of the house of bondage.

1. Thou shalt have on other gods before me.

2. Thou shalt not make unto thyself any graven image, nor the likeness of any thing that is in heaven above, or in the earth beneath, or in the water under the earth. Thou shalt not bow down thyself to them, nor serve them; for I, the Lord thy God, am a jealous God, visiting the iniquity of the fathers upon the children, unto the third and fourth generation of them that hate me, and showing mercy unto thousands of them that love me, and keep my commandments.

3. Thou shalt not take the name of the Lord thy God in vain; for the Lord will not hold him guiltless, that taketh his name in vain.

4. Remember the Sabbath day, to keep it holy; six days shalt thou labor and do all thy work; but the seventh day is the Sabbath of the Lord thy God; in it thou shalt do no manner of work, thou, nor thy son, nor thy daughter, thy man servant, nor thy maid servant, nor thy cattle, nor thy stranger that is within thy gates. For in six days the Lord made heaven and earth. The sea, and all that in them is, and rested the seventh day: wherefore the Lord blessed the Sabbath day, and hallowed it.

5. Honor thy father and thy mother, that thy days may be long in the land which the Lord thy God giveth thee.

6. Thou shalt not kill.

7. Thou shalt not commit adultery.

8. Thou shalt not steal.

9. Thou shalt not bear false witness against thy neighbor.

10. Thou shalt not covet thy neighbor's house; thou shalt not covet thy neighbor's wife, nor his man servant, not his maid servant, nor his ox, nor his ass, nor any thing that is thy neighbor's.

God gave His law to the children of Israel in the wilderness at Mount Sinai with great thundering and lightnings so that they feared for their lives. *"Wherefore then serveth the law? It was added because of transgressions, till the seed should come to whom the promise was made; and it was ordained by angels in the hand of a mediator. Wherefore the law was our schoolmaster to bring us unto Christ, that we might be justified by faith"* (Galatians 3:19 and 24). But above all, it is a law which reveals God's love for His people, and they in return show their love to Him by keeping the law. This is Jesus own words, *"The first of all the commandments is, Hear, O Israel; The Lord our God is one Lord: And thou shalt love the Lord thy God with all thy heart, and with all thy soul, and with all thy mind, and with all thy strength: this is the first commandment. And the second is like, namely this, Thou shalt love thy neighbour as thyself. There is none other commandment greater than these"* Mark 12:29-31). We shall dissect the law commandment by commandment in this light!

50.
The Division of God's Law

QUESTION: 93. How are these commandments divided?

ANSWER: Into two tables, the first of which teaches us how we must behave towards God; the second, what duties we own to our neighbor.

God called Moses into the Mount and talked with him face to face. He gave to Moses the two tables of the law which He wrote. "*And the LORD said unto Moses, Come up to me into the mount, and be there: and I will give thee tables of stone, and a law, and commandments which I have written; that thou mayest teach them.*" (Exodus 24:12). God not only gave them to Moses for the children of Israel, but God's law has been put into the heart of His people. "*But this shall be the covenant that I will make with the house of Israel; After those days, saith the LORD, I will put my law in their inward parts, and write it in their hearts; and will be their God, and they shall be my people*" (Jeremiah 31:33). The Law is divided into two sections of love. God requires us to love Him with our whole heart, nothing less will do! *"Jesus said unto him, Thou shalt love the Lord thy God with all thy heart, and with all thy soul, and with all thy mind. This is the first and great commandment"* (Matthew 22:37-38). This does not mean that we cannot love anyone or thing on earth, but love to God must come first. Anything less than this is an affront to the Triune God. This is why when persecution comes, that even at the expense of family, the Name of Jesus cannot be denied. Our love for the Lord is greater than all other loves.

The second table is also love on a horizontal level, so that we must love our neighbor. *"And the second is like unto it, Thou shalt love thy neighbour as thyself"* (Matthew 22:39). This flows out of the love of God shown to us, this we cannot do unless God is first in our lives. Without the Love of God we are selfish, thinking only of ourselves. *"Let nothing be done through strife or vainglory; but in lowliness of mind let each esteem other better than themselves. Look not every man on his own things, but every man also on the things of others. Let this mind be in you, which was also in Christ Jesus: Who, being in the form of God, thought it not robbery to be equal with God: But made himself of no reputation, and took upon him the form of a servant, and was made in the likeness of men: And being found in fashion as a man, he humbled himself, and became obedient unto death, even the death of the cross"* (Philippians 2:3-8). We will bring glory to God by our good works as God's love permeates every part of our lives. We return His love to Him by doing good to those around us. *"Then shall the King say unto them on his right hand, Come, ye blessed of my Father, inherit the kingdom prepared for you from the foundation of the world: For I* was an hungered, and ye gave me meat: I was thirsty, and ye gave me drink: I was a stranger, and ye took me in: Naked, and ye clothed me: I was sick, and ye visited me: I was in prison, and ye came unto me. Then shall the righteous answer him, saying, Lord, when saw we thee an hungered, and fed thee? or thirsty, and gave thee drink? When saw we thee a stranger, and took thee in? or naked, and clothed thee? Or when saw we thee sick, or in prison, and came unto thee? And the King shall answer and say unto them, Verily I say unto you, Inasmuch as ye have done it unto one of the least of these my brethren, ye have done it unto me" (Matthew 25:34-40).

51.
The First Commandment

QUESTION: 94. WHAT DOETH GOD rejoin in the first commandment?

ANSWER: THAT I, AS SINCERELY as I desire the salvation of my own soul, avoid and flee from all idolatry, sorcery, soothsaying, superstition, invocation of saints, or any other creature; and learn rightly to know the only true God; trust in him alone, learn humility and patience submit to him; expect all good things from him only; love, fear, and glorify him with my whole heart; as that I renounce and forsake all creatures, rather than commit even the least thing contrary to his will.

QUESTION: 95. WHAT IS IDOLATRY?

ANSWER: IDOLATRY IS, INSTEAD OF, or besides that one true God, who has manifested himself in his word, to contrive, or have any other object, in which men place their trust.

God, at Mt. Sinai reveals His love for His people by giving His law to them so they would show their love to Him in return by keeping His commandments. *"And God spake all these words, saying, I am the LORD thy God, which have brought thee out of the land of Egypt, out of the house of bondage"* (Exodus 20:1-2). God is saying, "Come my people. Come near and I will be your God and give you everything necessary for life and death. Only serve me with your whole heart." Our response should be to come with gratitude to Him for giving us His commandments. The desire of His people is to be able to live to His glory. Here we see two distinct groups of people. Natural man loves self and seeks to avoid God, but when the love of God is shed abroad in our heart; our love of self is turned into love for the God we sought to avoid before. *"And hope maketh not ashamed; because the love of God is shed abroad in our hearts by the Holy Ghost which is given unto us. For when we were yet without strength, in due time Christ died for the ungodly"* (Romans 5:5-6). All other gods become obstacles to us, so that even when we are threatened, we trust Him to give strength to overcome. *"And when they,* (captain with the officers) *had brought them,* (the apostles) *they set them before the council: and the high priest asked them, Saying, Did not we straitly command you that ye should not teach in this name? and, behold, ye have filled Jerusalem with your doctrine, and intend to bring this man's blood upon us. Then Peter and the other apostles answered and said, We ought to obey God rather than men"* (Acts 5:27-29). This first commandment is critical as we go through the other nine commandments, because if our love is not in this one only true God, Father, Son, and Holy Ghost we already break all of them every moment of every day. But more than that, we show in our action that the love of God is not in our heart. We are not born again! (Read John 3:1-20).

Thy wondrous testimonies, Lord,
my soul will keep and greatly praise;
Thy word, by faithful lips proclaimed,
to simplest minds the truth conveys.

O make Thy face to shine on me,
and teach me all Thy laws to keep;
Because Thy statutes are despised,
with overwhelming grief I weep.
Psalter 337:1 and 4 Taken from Psalm 119

52.
The Second Commandment

QUESTION: 96. WHAT DOTH GOD require in the second commandment?

ANSWER: THAT WE IN NO wise represent God by images, nor worship him in any other way than he has commanded in his word.

QUESTION: 97. ARE IMAGES THEN not at all to be made?

ANSWER: GOD NEITHER CAN, NOR may be represented, yet God forbids as to creatures; though they may be represented, yet God forbids to make, or have any resemblance of them either in order to worship them or to serve God by them.

QUESTION: 98. BUT MAY NOT images be tolerated in the churches, as books to the laity?

ANSWER: No: FOR WE MUST not pretend to be wiser than God, who will have his people taught, not by dumb images, but by the lively preaching of his word.

This image making flows out of our corrupt hearts. We want something to cling to of our own making. "*To whom then will ye liken God? or what likeness will ye compare unto him*" (Isaiah 40:18)? We want to worship the works of our own hands. What do these images look like? They are anything which we worship instead of the one only true God. By nature we worship, ourselves, our possessions, and any number of things that will perish. God's people also worship imagined images, our humility, our prayers, our tears and many other things which we use as reasons to impress God. God will have none of it, "*For I desired mercy, and not sacrifice; and the knowledge of God more than burnt offerings*" (Hosea 6:6). We have nothing to bring unto God, "*But we are all as an unclean thing, and all our righteousnesses are as filthy rags; and we all do fade as a leaf; and our iniquities, like the wind, have taken us away*" (Isaiah 64:6). So as in the first commandment, love is the motivating factor. Everything else will fall away, except Jesus Christ and His righteousness! With that we can live and with that we can die. Our prayer should be, "Give us that single eye Thy name to glorify." It is His Word that the Spirit uses to reveal the One we must bow down to and His Name is Jesus Christ, who is everything needed for this life and a better. "*For unto us a child is born, unto us a son is given: and the government shall be upon his shoulder: and his name shall be called Wonderful, Counsellor, The mighty God, The everlasting Father, The Prince of Peace. Of the increase of his government and peace there shall be no end, upon the throne of David, and upon his kingdom, to order it, and to establish it with judgment and with justice from henceforth even for ever.*

The zeal of the LORD of hosts will perform this" (Isaiah 9:6-7). This God gives this to us through the preaching of His Word by faithful ministers. Nothing more is needed! We were created in God's image, which we have cast off, but by the Cross of Calvary that image was restored. Do you reflect that image by the grace of God? That is the only image we need!

53.
The Third Commandment

QUESTION: 99. WHAT IS REQUIRED in the third commandment?

ANSWER: THAT WE, NOT ONLY by cursing or perjury, but also by rash swearing, must not profane or abuse the name of God; nor by silence or connivance be partakers of these horrible sins in others; and, briefly, that we use the holy name of God no otherwise than with fear and reverence; so that he may be rightly confessed and worshipped by us, and be glorified in all our words and works.

QUESTION: 100. Is THEN THE profaning of God's name by swearing and cursing, so heinous a sin, that his wrath is kindled against those who do not endeavor, as much as in them lies, to prevent and forbid such cursing and swearing?

ANSWER: IT UNDOUBTEDLY IS, FOR there is no sin greater or more provoking to God, than the profaning of his name; and therefore he has commanded this sin to be punished with death.

The breaching of this commandment is a direct affront to God. There is cursing and swearing all around us every day. It is as if man is asking God to cast them into hell by all the cursing and swearing, which is in reality a prayer to do just that. Many times we hear it and cringe, but don't say anything, giving the excuse that we are just casting pearls before swine. (Read Matthew 7:6). But this is just an excuse to ease our conscience; this makes us guilty as well! *"Whosoever therefore shall confess me before men, him will I confess also before my Father which is in heaven. But whosoever shall deny me before men, him will I also deny before my Father which is in heaven"* (Mathew 10:32-33). O, the love of God, for His people as He reveals this love to them through the commandments. There is a reward for those who keep them, but also punishment for those who do not. We all fail every day, and this commandment condemns us. What shall we do? I read an encouragement in these words, (as much as in them lies). How can this be an encouragement? *"My little children, these things write I unto you, that ye sin not. And if any man sin, we have an advocate with the Father, Jesus Christ the righteous: And he is the propitiation for our sins: and not for ours only, but also for the sins of the whole world"* (1 John 2:1-2). The only hope for us as commandment breakers is to flee to the Commandment Keeper, (Jesus Christ the righteous). Our only hope is His blood and righteousness. *"Surely, shall one say, in the LORD have I righteousness and strength: even to him shall men come; and all that are incensed against him shall be ashamed. In the LORD shall all the seed of Israel be justified, and shall glory"* (Isaiah 45:24-25).

Without Him our punishment is eternal death, but in Him we have eternal life.

The living God in righteousness will recompense with shame
The men who, hardened by success, forget to fear His Name.
Psalter 149:3 Taken from Psalm 55

54.
The Third Commandment expanded

QUESTION: 101. MAY WE THEN swear religiously by the name of God?

ANSWER: YES: EITHER WHEN THE magistrates demand it of the subjects, or when necessity requires us thereby to confirm fidelity and truth to the glory of God, and the safety of our neighbor: for such an oath is founded on God's word, and therefore was justly used by the saints, both in the Old and New Testament.

QUESTION: 102. MAY WE ALSO swear by saints or any other creature?

ANSWER: No; FOR A LAWFUL oath is calling upon God, as the only one who knows the heart, that he will bear witness to the truth, and punish me if I swear falsely; which is due to no creature.

Cursing and swearing in most cases is taking God's name in vain, but there is a different side to swearing which is used by governments or other organizations to install men into office. This is called swearing an oath. This calls heaven and earth to record that what is being done is confirming truth, as in a trial, so that men do not receive unjust sentence for crimes they did not commit. Men elected into office are installed and give an oath of allegiance on the bible. These are all legitimate swearing. *"For men verily swear by the greater: and an oath for confirmation is to them an end of all strife"* (Hebrews 6:16). In these oaths, God receives the glory and may be used. To use anything but God's Word for making an oath or swearing is an abomination which God will judge accordingly. To whom do you give your allegiance? God gave oath swearing to us because of our sinful nature, which without His word, would fail in being truthful. Oath swearing calls us to account so that we would realize that God is in control of us and our neighbor's lives. *"Again, ye have heard that it hath been said by them of old time, Thou shalt not forswear thyself, but shalt perform unto the Lord thine oaths: But I say unto you, Swear not at all; neither by heaven; for it is God's throne: Nor by the earth; for it is his footstool: neither by Jerusalem; for it is the city of the great King. Neither shalt thou swear by thy head, because thou canst not make one hair white or black. But let your communication be, Yea, yea; Nay, nay: for whatsoever is more than these cometh of evil"* (Matthew 5:33-37). In this too we see the love of God to third commandment breakers. Let us treat our neighbors as we would be treated, loving them. *"Beloved, if God so loved us, we ought also to love one another. No man hath seen*

God at any time. If we love one another, God dwelleth in us, and his love is perfected in us. Hereby know we that we dwell in him, and he in us, because he hath given us of his Spirit" (1 John 4:11-13).

55.
The Fourth Commandment

QUESTION: 103. WHAT DOES GOD require in the fourth commandment?

ANSWER: FIRST, THAT THE MINISTRY of the gospel and the schools be maintained; and that I. especially on the Sabbath, that is on the day of rest, diligently frequent the church of God, to hear His word, to use the sacraments, publicly to call upon the Lord, and contribute to the relief of the poor, as becomes a christian. Secondly, that all the days of my life I cease from my evil works, and yield myself to the Lord, to work by his Holy Spirit in me: and thus begin in this life the eternal Sabbath.

God, after He created the world in six day, saw a perfect creation. Everything reflected His glory. There was nothing left to do. It was finished. "*Thus the heavens and the earth were finished, and all the host of them. And on the seventh day God ended his work which he had made; and he rested on the seventh day from all his work which he had made. And God blessed the seventh day, and sanctified it: because that in it he had rested from all his work which God created and made"* (Genesis 2:1-3). The Sabbath becomes a day which we look forward to, an oasis in this wilderness of sin that we live in. It is a giving our body and soul to God as our faithful Savior and Lord in complete submission. Today our Sabbath is called the Lord's Day. It was a looking forward to the coming of the Messiah, but now a rejoicing in the risen Lord our Savior. The three fold cord of home, church, and school must work together to bind us to God's Word for His glory. God's house should be our delight because it is the place He has promised to bless. We work in the world six days a week to support our families and the propagation of the gospel to the coming of God's kingdom. *"I exhort therefore, that, first of all, supplications, prayers, intercessions, and giving of thanks, be made for all men; For kings, and for all that are in authority; that we may lead a quiet and peaceable life in all godliness and honesty"* (1 Timothy 2:1-2). When God, (in Jesus Christ) is our only comfort, we long for everyone to hear the gospel, to find comfort themselves through the preaching and the use of the sacraments. *"For whatsoever is born of God overcometh the world: and this is the victory that overcometh the world, even our faith. Who is he that overcometh the world, but he that believeth that Jesus is the Son of God"* (1 John 5:4-5)? Are you looking for the consummation of the eternal Sabbath when Jesus Christ shall come on the clouds to judge the world in righteousness? Do you have the garment of His righteousness? Do you see the fourth commandment as given to us for our comfort, or does it make you uncomfortable? *"And we know that we are of God, and the whole world lieth in wickedness. And we know that the Son of God is come, and hath given us an understanding, that we may know him that is true, and we are in him that is true, even in his Son Jesus Christ. This is the true God, and eternal life*" (1 John 5:19-20).

56.
The Fifth Commandment

QUESTION: 104. WHAT DOTH GOD require in the fifth commandment?

ANSWER: THAT I SHOW ALL honor, love and fidelity, to my father and mother, and all in authority over me, and submit myself to their good instruction, and correction, with due obedience; and also patiently bear with their weaknesses and infirmities, since it pleases God to govern us by their hand.

As our teacher leads us into the fifth commandment, the scene switches to the horizontal. "*Thou shalt love thy neighbour as thyself*" (Romans 13:9b). The first four focused on how God is to be served. The Lord is a God of order explaining to us how our lives are to be ordered. The basic form is family. God created man and made woman for a help meet for him. From this union children would be born which would love and honor their parents as to the Lord with a promise. "*Children, obey your parents in the Lord: for this is right. Honour thy father and mother; which is the first commandment with promise; That it may be well with thee, and thou mayest live long on the earth*" (Ephesians 6:1-2). The command to honor father and mother goes into every sphere of our lives. We must honor those over us at our work, in church, and all others who have authority over us. "*Servants, be obedient to them that are your masters according to the flesh, with fear and trembling, in singleness of your heart, as unto Christ; Not with eyeservice, as menpleasers; but as the servants of Christ, doing the will of God from the heart; With good will doing service, as to the Lord, and not to men: Knowing that whatsoever good thing any man doeth, the same shall he receive of the Lord, whether he be bond or free*" (Ephesians 6:5-8). Our Lord Jesus Christ, Himself was obedient to His Father saying, "*I can of mine own self do nothing: as I hear, I judge: and my judgment is just; because I seek not mine own will, but the will of the Father which hath sent me*" (John 5:30). Again this commandment brings out the love of the Triune God in bringing law breakers to Himself through the Law Keeper, Jesus Christ.

> The off'ring on the altar burned gives no delight to Thee;
> The hearing ear the willing heart, Thou givest unto me.

> Then, O my God, I come, I come, Thy purpose to fulfill;
> They law is written in my heart, 'tis joy to do Thy will.

> Before Thy people I will now Thy righteousness proclaim;
> Thou knowest, Lord, I will not cease to praise Thy holy Name.

> I never have within my heart Thy faithfulness concealed,
> But Thy salvation and Thy truth to men I have revealed.
> Psalter 109 Taken from Psalm 40

57.
The Sixth Commandment

QUESTION: 105. WHAT DOTH GOD require in the sixth commandment?

ANSWER: THAT NEITHER IN THOUGHTS, nor words, nor gestures, much less in deeds, I dishonor, hate, wound, or kill my neighbor by myself or by another; but that I lay aside all desire of revenge: also, that I hurt not myself, nor wilfully expose myself to any danger. Wherefore also the magistrate is armed with the sword to prevent murder.

QUESTION: 106. BUT THIS COMMANDMENT seems only to speak of murder?

ANSWER: IN FORBIDDING MURDER, GOD teaches us, that He abhors the causes thereof, such as envy, hatred, anger, and desire of revenge; and that He accounts all these as murder.

QUESTION: 107. BUT IS IT enough that we do not kill any man in the manner mentioned above?

ANSWER: No: FOR WHEN GOD forbids envy, hatred, and anger, He commands us to love our neighbor as ourselves; to show patience, peace, meekness, mercy, and all kindness, towards him, and prevent his hurt as much as in us lies; and that we do good, even to our enemies.

To take another's life is a very serious thing! Daily we hear of killings and it is looked upon as the ultimate sin. Murder is spilling the blood of a creature God has created to glorify Him. In many places the death penalty is given for this crime. "*Ye have heard that it was said by them of old time, Thou shalt not kill; and whosoever shall kill shall be in danger of the judgment: But I say unto you, That whosoever is angry with his brother without a cause shall be in danger of the judgment: and whosoever shall say to his brother, Raca, shall be in danger of the council: but whosoever shall say, Thou fool, shall be in danger of hell fire*" (Matthew 5:21-22). The police will go to great lengths to find the killer. This commandment extends much farther than killing, even to hate someone or to be angry, thinking they have things which they do not deserve. This is envy. "*For the wrath of man worketh not the righteousness of God*" (James 1:20). Suicide is murder, and humanly speaking, they work their own condemnation, as there is no time for repentance. "*Envyings, murders, drunkenness, revellings, and such like: of the which I tell you before, as I have also told you in time past, that they which do such things shall not inherit the kingdom of God*" (Galatians 5:21). The sixth commandment goes even deeper; to even have thought to do it Jesus said is <u>murder</u>. God created us good and upright, perfect in every way. The sin committed by our first parents was they wanted to be like God! They were

<u>envious!</u> This shows that instead of loving God above all, and our neighbor as our self, we only think of our self, and thereby all the commandments are broken. The law is given by God to humble us before Him in repentance seeking forgiveness. It is a lack of love; which only God in Jesus Christ, through the working of the Holy Ghost, can give us. The question comes back! What is thy only comfort in life and in death? Without this you and I are nothing more than self murders who cannot inherit eternal life. The blood of Jesus Christ is the only remedy that will do.

58.
The Seventh Commandment

QUESTION: 108. WHAT DOTH THE seventh commandment teach us?

ANSWER: THAT ALL UNCLEANNESS IS accursed of God: and that therefore we must with all our hearts detest the same, and live chastely and temperately, whether in holy wedlock, or in single life.

QUESTION: 109. DOTH GOD FORBID in this commandment, only adultery, and such like gross sins?

ANSWER: SINCE BOTH OUR BODY and soul are temples of the Holy Ghost, He commands is to preserve them pure and holy: therefore He forbids all unchaste action, gestures, words, thoughts, desires, and whatever can entice men thereto.

In today's world, the seventh commandment is looked upon as just a normal human response! It's no big deal, everyone is doing it! Everywhere you look sexual scenes are used to excite our animal desires. God created us good and upright, and this desire was also part of our created being. Sin has entered this world. We are sinners and if left to ourselves will lust ourselves straight into hell. "*Know ye not that the unrighteous shall not inherit the kingdom of God? Be not deceived: neither fornicators, nor idolaters, nor adulterers, nor effeminate, nor abusers of themselves with mankind, Nor thieves, nor covetous, nor drunkards, nor revilers, nor extortioners, shall inherit the kingdom of God*" (1 Corinthians 6:9-10). The sin against the seventh commandment is especially accursed of God because we were created to glorify Him with our whole being. God says, "*Be ye holy for I am holy*" (1 Peter 1:16b). This is true not only with the illicit sex act, but sexual suggestions, our thoughts, anything that will entice or liven our desires outside of the bounds that God has set. God, in Paradise, before men fell, has instituted marriage of one man and one woman. This beautiful union was given to man as the way to glorify God, and outside of this union, it is sin. "*Marriage is honourable in all, and the bed undefiled: but whoremongers and adulterers God will judge*" (Hebrews 13:4). It is no wonder that this commandment is so grossly broken. Man is in rebellion against God and all His commandments. We will not have Him to be our God. All but those drawn from the darkness of sin, learn to love Him and His law because of the cost, which Jesus Christ paid to save them from the curse of the law. They sorrow because of their sin and repent, fleeing to Him to be freed from it. "*What? know ye not that your body is the temple of the Holy Ghost which is in you, which ye have of God, and ye are not your own? For ye are bought with a price: therefore glorify God in your body, and in your spirit, which are God's"* (1 Corinthians 6:19-20). This commandment again brings us back to the first question, "What is thy only comfort in life and in death"? It is the love of God for His people that they will be kept by him. *"I will build my church; and the gates of hell shall not prevail against it"* (Matthew 16:18b). This is our only hope for this time, but also for all eternity. Do you love God's law?

59.
The Eighth Commandment

QUESTION: 110. WHAT DOTH GOD forbid in the eighth commandment?

ANSWER: GOD FORBIDS, NOT ONLY those thefts and robberies, which are punishable by the magistrate; but he comprehends under the name of theft all wicked tricks and devices, whereby we design to appropriate to ourselves the goods which belong to our neighbor: whether it be by force, or under the appearance of right, as by unjust weights, ells, measures, fraudulent merchandise, false coins, usury, or by any other way forbidden by God; as also all covetousness, all abuse and waste of His gifts.

QUESTION: 111. BUT WHAT DOTH God require in this commandment?

ANSWER: THAT I PROMOTE THE advantage of my neighbor in every instance I can or may; and deal with him as I desire to be dealt with by others: further also that I faithfully labor, so that I may be able to relieve the needy.

When we see the depth of our fall we can but say, "*What is man, that thou art mindful of him? or the son of man, that thou visitest him*" (Hebrews 2:6b). Sin and corruption seems to fill the whole world, and righteousness is non-existent. There is no love for our neighbor, but every man is for himself. Yet even this commandment is put into the section of gratitude by our instructor! How can that be? This takes us back to the creation where God made all things perfect. Man loved God with his whole heart, mind, and soul. Satan, as a thief, came into the garden of God with enticing words and stole the heart of man, filling it with evil against God and his fellow man. But God! Who from all eternity had covenanted with Himself, that His Son, (our Lord Jesus Christ) would come into the world in the fullness of time as the Son of man to buy back a people known only to Him, setting them free from the bondage of sin, defeating Satan once and for all at Calvary's Cross. "*I have glorified thee on the earth: I have finished the work which thou gavest me to do*" (John 17:4). The wonder is brought home to His people's heart, that thieves could be reconciled into favor with God by the shed blood of Jesus Christ without any merit of their own. God's love for them fills them with gratitude and they in turn love Him and their neighbor by treating them as they would like to be treated. Though there are many thieves in the world, God's people grieve that they steal from Him by spending so much of their time not glorifying Him. This again begs the question; "What is thy only comfort in life and in death?"

As Thou, O Lord,
hast made me strong to overcome my mighty foe,
So now to fight against the wrong and conquer in Thy Name I go.

Jehovah lives, and blest is He, my rock, my refuge and defense,
My Saviour Who delivers me, and will the wicked recompense.

For grace and mercy ever near,
for foes subdued and victories won,
All nations of the earth shall hear my praise
for what the Lord has done.

ANON

60.
The Ninth Commandment

QUESTION: 112. WHAT IS REQUIRED in the ninth commandment?

ANSWER: THAT I BEAR FALSE witness against no man, nor falsify any man's words; that I be no backbiter, nor slanderer; or I do not judge, nor join in condemning any man rashly, or unheard; but that I avoid all sorts of lies and deceit, as the proper works of the devil, unless I would bring down upon me the heavy wrath of God; likewise, that in judgment and all other dealings I love the truth, speak it uprightly and confess it; also that I defend and promote, as much as I am able, the honor and good character of my neighbor.

As we go down the list of commandments, the law burrows deeper and deeper into our hearts. God would expose our iniquities and bring us as Job to confess, *"I have heard of thee by the hearing of the ear: but now mine eye seeth thee. Wherefore I abhor myself, and repent in dust and ashes"* (Job 42"5-6). Our hearts are so deceitful, that as we expose or talk about others we try to justify ourselves. Again we see the ninth commandment given to make us search our hearts and bring us to repentance before God. This is love. God deals with every one of His people personally, He does not need our help. *"Judge not, that ye be not judged. For with what judgment ye judge, ye shall be judged: and with what measure ye mete, it shall be measured to you again. And why beholdest thou the mote that is in thy brother's eye, but considerest not the beam that is in thine own eye? Or how wilt thou say to thy brother, Let me pull out the mote out of thine eye; and, behold, a beam is in thine own eye"* (Matthew 7:1-4)? Lying is Satan forte; he is the master liar. As we are his by nature to lie is like our second nature. As long as he can have us imitate him he does not bother us. Our tongues are a world of iniquity as James says. We cannot tame them, but there is One who can! Jesus Christ, the Righteous. He never spoke one untruth, only speaking gracious words as He walked here on earth. We need to be born again completely; God does not do a half work, but will finish what He has begun. Without Him there is no rest, (comfort). Let us guard our hearts because, *"A good man out of the good treasure of his heart bringeth forth that which is good; and an evil man out of the evil treasure of his heart bringeth forth that which is evil: for of the abundance of the heart his mouth speaketh"* (Luke 6:45).

61.
The Tenth Commandment

QUESTION: 113. WHAT DOTH THE tenth commandment require of us?

ANSWER: THAT EVEN THE SMALLEST inclination or thought, contrary to any of God's commandments, never rise in our hearts; but that at all times we hate all sin with our whole heart and delight in all righteousness.

QUESTION: 114. BUT CAN THOSE who are converted to God perfectly keep these commandments?

ANSWER. NO; BUT EVEN THE holiest men, while in this life, have only a small beginning of this obedience; yet so, that with a sincere resolution they begin to live, not only according to some, but all the commandments of God.

Jesus said that nothing of the law will ever pass away. "*And it is easier for heaven and earth to pass, than one tittle of the law to fail*" (Luke 16:17). The law makes sin to be sin. "*What shall we say then? is the law sin? God forbid. Nay, I had not known sin, but by the law: for I had not known lust, except the law had said, Thou shalt not covet"* (Romans 7:7). The Holy Ghost opens our heart to see the exceeding sinfulness of sin. *"Was then that which is good made death unto me? God forbid. But sin, that it might appear sin, working death in me by that which is good; that sin by the commandment might become exceeding sinful. For we know that the law is spiritual: but I am carnal, sold under sin"* (Romans 7:13-14). We learn what covetous people we are. What we have is not enough to keep us satisfied. We always want more. God is teaching us that what we call our own does not belongs to us, but is only a gift from God. "Not that I speak in respect of want: for I have learned, in whatsoever state I am, therewith to be content" (Philippians 4:11). God knows how to bring us to trust only in Him for all things, and not only trust Him, but to be content with what He gives. To know and to be known of God is everything. We can have every temporal thing here and in reality have nothing if He is not our God. We thank God for all His blessing to us, and we thank Him if He takes them away. *"I know both how to be abased, and I know how to abound: every where and in all things I am instructed both to be full and to be hungry, both to abound and to suffer need. I can do all things through Christ which strengtheneth me"* (Philippians 4:12-13). The law affords no comfort. The law Keeper, (Jesus Christ), came and bore the penalty so that law breakers would be pronounced free.

Deceit and falsehood I abhor, but love thy law,

Thy truth revealed;

My steadfast hope is in thy word;

Thou art my refuge and my shield;

The paths of sin I have not trod,

but kept the precepts of my God.

According to Thy gracious word uphold me,

Lord, deliver me;

O do not let me be ashamed of patient hope and trust in Thee;

Uphold me, and I shall stand and ever follow Thy command.

Psalter 335 1- 2. Taken from Psalm 119

62.
God's Conforming Work

QUESTION: 115. WHY WILL GOD then have the Ten Commandments so strictly preached, since no man in this life can keep them?

First, that all our lifetime we may learn more and more to know our sinful nature, and thus become the more earnest in seeking the remission of sin, and righteousness in Christ; likewise, that we constantly endeavor and pray to God for the grace of the Holy Spirit, that we may become more and more conformable to the image of God, till we arrive at the perfection proposed to us, in a life to come.

God will have a people and they shall praise Him! This would not be possible without the law work of the Holy Spirit in His people's heart. As the Triune God works in the heart, the love of God in Jesus Christ becomes evident in them. It makes enemies friends. It makes sinners saints, and the world becomes enemy territory. The seed planted grows because the soil of the heart has been prepared to receive it. "*That ye put off concerning the former conversation the old man, which is corrupt according to the deceitful lusts; And be renewed in the spirit of your mind; And that ye put on the new man, which after God is created in righteousness and true holiness"* (Ephesians 4:22-24). The law becomes precious because the One who gave it is now Lord of our life. "*O how love I thy law! it is my meditation all the day.*" (Psalm 119:97). The law becomes the rule and guide of our life. "*Thy word is a lamp unto my feet, and a light unto my path*" (Psalm 119:105). We need this Word to guide us, because of our proneness to wander. Our heart cries out to Him, (Jesus Christ) who said, *I am the way, the truth, and the life: no man cometh unto the Father, but by me*" (John 14:6). With the Psalmist we cry, "O, Lord keep me near Thy side, for near Thee all is well." This is the only comfort in life and in death because, "*The LORD will perfect that which concerneth me: thy mercy, O LORD, endureth for ever: forsake not the works of thine own hands*" (Psalm 138:8).

O Lord, by Thee delivered, I Thee with song extol;
My foes Thou hast not suffered to glory o'er my fall.
O Lord, my God, I sought Thee, and Thou didst heal and save;
Thou, Lord, from death didst ransom and keep me from the grave.

My grief is turned to gladness, to Thee my thanks I raise,
Who hast removed my sorrow and girded me with praise;
And now, no longer silent, my heart Thy praise will sing;
O Lord, my God, forever my thanks to Thee I bring.
Psalter 77:1 and 4. Taken from Psalm 30

63.
Thankfulness Expressed

QUESTION: 116. WHY IS PRAYER necessary for Christians?

ANSWER: BECAUSE IT IS THE chief part of thankfulness which God requires of us: and also, because God will give His grace and Holy Spirit to those only, who with sincere desires continually ask them of Him, and are thankful for them.

QUESTION: 117. WHAT ARE THE requisites of this prayer, which is acceptable to God, and which He will hear?

ANSWER: FIRST, THAT WE FROM the heart pray to the one true God only, who hath manifested Himself in His word, for all things, He hath commanded us to ask of Him; secondly, that so we may deeply humble ourselves in the presence of His divine majesty; thirdly, that we be fully persuaded that He, notwithstanding that we are unworthy of it, for the sake of Christ our Lord, certainly hear our prayer, as He has promised us in His word.

Communication is a necessary part of our existence. God has given us His word so that we would understand who He is and what is required or expected of us. We in turn would make our needs known to God, "*And I say unto you, Ask, and it shall be given you; seek, and ye shall find; knock, and it shall be opened unto you. For every one that asketh receiveth; and he that seeketh findeth; and to him that knocketh it shall be opened*" (Luke 11:9-10). God is all knowing and yet would be inquired of by His children. "*Therefore take no thought, saying, What shall we eat? or, What shall we drink? or, Wherewithal shall we be clothed? (For after all these things do the Gentiles seek:) for your heavenly Father knoweth that ye have need of all these things. But seek ye first the kingdom of God, and his righteousness; and all these things shall be added unto you*" (Matthew 6:32-33). God has promised to have His ear open for the cries of His people. "*Offer unto God thanksgiving; and pay thy vows unto the most High: And call upon me in the day of trouble: I will deliver thee, and thou shalt glorify me*" (Psalm 50:14-15). Prayer honors God and brings us before Him in humility. God does not answer us because of our prayers, but because of who He is. He loves us as His children in His Son Jesus Christ, "*Like as a father pitieth his children, so the LORD pitieth them that fear him*" (Psalm 103:14). God, in Jesus Christ, is a prayer giving, prayer hearing, and prayer answering God. Our prayers are stained with sin, but Jesus Christ takes them and washes them in His blood making them presentable before His Father. Everything we do and say must be for Christ's sake or they cannot be heard. "*Whatsoever ye shall ask the Father in my name, he will give it you. Hitherto have ye asked nothing in my name: ask, and ye shall receive, that your joy may be full. For the Father himself loveth you, because ye have loved me, and have believed that I came out from God*" (John 16:24-25, and26). This is comfort in life here. God will hear the cries of the needy. "*For he shall deliver the needy when he crieth; the poor also, and him that hath no helper. He shall spare the poor and needy, and shall save the souls of the needy*" (Psalm 72:12-13).

64.
Beggars Satisfied

QUESTION: 118. WHAT HATH GOD commanded us to ask Him?

ANSWER: ALL THINGS NECESSARY FOR soul and body; which Christ our Lord has comprised in that prayer He Himself has taught us.

QUESTION: 119. WHAT ARE THE words of that prayer?

ANSWER: OUR FATHER WHICH ART in heaven, Hallowed be Thy name. Thy kingdom come. Thy will be done on earth as it is in heaven. Give us this day our daily bread. And lead us not into temptation, but deliver us from evil. For Thine is the kingdom, and the power, and the glory, for ever. Amen.

God commands men everywhere to pray, "*And that every tongue should confess that Jesus Christ is Lord, to the glory of God the Father. Wherefore, my beloved, as ye have always obeyed, not as in my presence only, but now much more in my absence, work out your own salvation with fear and trembling. For it is God which worketh in you both to will and to do of his good pleasure"* (Philippians 2:11-13). God commands and then gives the strength to obey by the Holy Spirit. *"Likewise the Spirit also helpeth our infirmities: for we know not what we should pray for as we ought: but the Spirit itself maketh intercession for us with groanings which cannot be uttered. And he that searcheth the hearts knoweth what is the mind of the Spirit, because he maketh intercession for the saints according to the will of God"* (Romans 8:26-27). God, who knows we are prayerless by nature, plants His love in our hearts and makes it His dwelling place, giving us words and desire to pray according to His will. *"And I will pray the Father, and he shall give you another Comforter, that he may abide with you for ever; Even the Spirit of truth; whom the world cannot receive, because it seeth him not, neither knoweth him: but ye know him; for he dwelleth with you, and shall be in you"* (John 14:16-17). There is nothing that will satisfy the soul except Him!

O God, most holy are Thy ways,
and who like Thee deserves my praise?
Thou only doest wondrous things,
the whole wide world Thy glory sings;
Thy outstretched arm Thy people saved,
Tho' sore distressed and long enslaved.

O God, from Thee the waters fled,
the depths were moved with mighty dread;
The swelling clouds their torrents poured,
and o'er the earth the tempest roared;

'Mid lightning's flash and thunder sound great
trembling shock the solid ground.

Thy way was in the sea, O God,
Thro mighty waters, deep and broad;
None understood but God alone,
to man Thy footsteps were unknown;
But safe Thy people Thou didst keep,
Almighty Shepherd of Thy sheep.
Psalter 211, Taken from Psalm 77

This greatness experienced by God's people, brings prayers of thanksgiving to Him, who said, "*I will never leave thee, nor forsake thee. So that we may boldly say, The Lord is my helper, and I will not fear what man shall do unto me*" (Hebrews 13:5b-6).

65.
God Our Father

QUESTION: 120. WHY HATH CHRIST commanded us to address God thus: "Our Father"?

ANSWER: THAT IMMEDIATELY, IN THE very beginning of our prayer, He might excite in us a childlike reverence for, and confidence in God, which are the foundation of our prayer: namely, that God is become our Father in Christ, and will much less deny us what we ask of Him in true faith, than our parents will refuse us earthly things.

QUESTION: 121. WHY IS IT here added, "Which art in heaven:?

ANSWER: LEST WE SHOULD FORM any earthly conception of God's heavenly majesty, and that we may expect from His almighty power all things necessary for soul and body.

God as our Father in creation has a right to expect us to reverence Him as Father. The problem is not with God as our

Father, but with us as His children. We have left Him, turned our back on Him, and chosen Satan as our father in the sin of our earthly father Adam. *"Jesus said unto them, If God were your Father, ye would love me: for I proceeded forth and came from God; neither came I of myself, but he sent me. Why do ye not understand my speech? even because ye cannot hear my word. Ye are of your father the devil, and the lusts of your father ye will do. He was a murderer from the beginning, and abode not in the truth, because there is no truth in him. When he speaketh a lie, he speaketh of his own: for he is a liar, and the father of it"* (John 8:42-44). This is what brings the great enmity of God being our Father. Satan is only our step father! Through God's Word we know better so we try to bury the thought to ease our conscience. God, as Father has provided all things for us even when we denied Him as our Father. God will not forsake His people. He will gather them and restore His family to be a Father unto them. *"Since thou wast precious in my sight, thou hast been honourable, and I have loved thee: therefore will I give men for thee, and people for thy life. Fear not: for I am with thee: I will bring thy seed from the east, and gather thee from the west; I will say to the north, Give up; and to the south, Keep not back: bring my sons from far, and my daughters from the ends of the earth; Even every one that is called by my name: for I have created him for my glory, I have formed him; yea, I have made him"* (Isaiah 43:4-7). The love of God will humble them in the dust as they see this glorious and majestic God to be their Father. They willingly follow Him fully. *"Asshur shall not save us; we will not ride upon horses: neither will we say any more to the work of our hands, Ye are our gods: for in thee the fatherless findeth mercy. I will heal their backsliding, I will love them freely: for mine anger is turned away from him*" (Hosea 14:3-4). Then we will pray to Him as, "Our Father which art in heaven." It is our only comfort in life and in death that I do not belong to myself, but to my faithful Savior Jesus Christ, as the Catechism begins.

66.
Hallowing God's Name

QUESTION: 122. WHICH IS THE first petition?

ANSWER: "HALLOWED BE THY NAME"; grant us, first, rightly to know Thee, and to sanctify. Glorify, and praise Thee, in all Thy works, in which Thy power, wisdom, goodness, justice, mercy and truth, are clearly displayed; and further also, that we may so order and direct our whole lives, our thought, words and actions, that Thy name may never be blasphemed, but rather honored and praised on our account.

To hallow a thing is to regard it as holy or sacred. God must be acknowledged as holy, putting man in submission to Him. Even the angels are not pure in His sight. The vision Isaiah had filled Him with awe, "*I saw also the Lord sitting upon a throne, high and lifted up, and his train filled the temple. Above it stood the seraphims: each one had six wings; with twain he covered his face, and with twain he covered his feet, and with twain he did fly. And one cried unto another, and said, Holy, holy, holy, is the*

LORD of hosts: the whole earth is full of his glory" (Isaiah 6:1b-3). What a display of God's power, wisdom, and justice, "*Then said I, (*Isaiah), *Woe is me! for I am undone; because I am a man of unclean lips, and I dwell in the midst of a people of unclean lips: for mine eyes have seen the King, the LORD of hosts*" (Isaiah 6:5). Thankfully there is also goodness, mercy, and truth because of the sacrifice. "*Then flew one of the seraphims unto me, having a live coal in his hand, which he had taken with the tongs from off the altar: And he laid it upon my mouth, and said, Lo, this hath touched thy lips; and thine iniquity is taken away, and thy sin purged*" (Isaiah 6:6-7). The coal off the altar represents the bloody sacrifice of Jesus Christ. "*Him hath God exalted with his right hand to be a Prince and a Saviour, for to give repentance to Israel, and forgiveness of sins*" (Acts 5:31). This Sacrifice gives the death worthy sinner an audience with the holy, righteous, and just God and live! A holy Triune God and a sinner are reconciled forever. This God is larger than the creation itself. "*But made himself of no reputation, and took upon him the form of a servant, and was made in the likeness of men: And being found in fashion as a man, he humbled himself, and became obedient unto death, even the death of the cross*" (Philippians 2:7-8). This God deserves honor and praise as King and Lord over all. He will bring His people to Himself, and destroy all His enemies forever. What is your only comfort in life and in death?

67.
The Kingdom of God

QUESTION: 123. WHICH IS THE second petition?

ANSWER: "THY KINGDOM COME"; THAT is, rule us so by Thy word and Spirit, that we may submit ourselves more and more to Thee; preserve and increase Thy church; destroy the works of the devil, and all violence which would exalt itself against Thee; and also, all wicked counsels devised against Thy holy word; till the full perfection of Thy kingdom take place, wherein Thou shalt be all in all.

Christ told His disciples that He would ascend up to His Father, but would come again to receive them and all His people unto Himself. *"In my Father's house are many mansions: if it were not so, I would have told you. I go to prepare a place for you. And if I go and prepare a place for you, I will come again, and receive you unto myself; that where I am, there ye may be also."* (John 14:2-3). What a great anticipation for His people as they travel through the world as pilgrims! *"Looking unto Jesus the author and finisher of our faith; who for the joy that was set before him endured the cross, despising the shame, and is set down at the right hand of the throne of God"* (Hebrews 12:2). God His Father has put all things into His hand, ruling and directing all things to His honor and glory for the good of His people. To know Him, (Jesus) is life eternal, but not to know Him is death. *"But let him that glorieth glory in this, that he understandeth and knoweth me, that I am the LORD which exercise lovingkindness, judgment, and righteousness, in the earth: for in these things I delight, saith the LORD"* (Jeremiah 9:24).

> Christ shall have dominion over land and sea,
> Earth's remotest regions shall His empire be;
> They that wilds inhabit shall their worship bring,
> Kings shall render tribute, Nations serve our King.

> When the needy seek Him, He will mercy show;
> Yea, the weak and helpless shall His pity know;
> He will surely save them from oppression's might,
> For their lives are precious in His holy sight.

> Ever and forever shall His Name endure,
> Long as suns continue it shall stand secure;
> And in Him forever all men shall be blest,
> And all nations hail Him King of kings confessed.

> Unto God Almighty joyful Zion sings;
> He alone is glorious, dong wonderous things,
> Ever-more, ye people, bless His glorious Name,
> His eternal glory thro' the earth proclaim.
> Psalter 200, Taken from Psalm 72

Do you know this King? He is coming again to take His people to Himself, and they shall behold His glory, but those who do not know Him He will destroy! "*And the God of peace shall bruise Satan under your feet shortly. The grace of our Lord Jesus Christ be with you. Amen*" (Romans 16:20).

68.
Bowing under God's Will

QUESTION: 124. WHICH IS THE third petition?

ANSWER: "THY WILL BE DONE on earth as it is in heaven"; that is, grant that we and all men may renounce our own will, and without murmuring obey Thy will, which is only good; that so every one may attend to, and perform the duties of His station and calling, as willingly and faithfully as the angels do in heaven.

This is the one petition most often neglected in our prayers! Even though we do not say it we want God to see it our way, and do it for our sake! The only thing that happens for our sake is to be forgotten eternally by God. Hell and destruction is the best thing we can hope for without God's will. "*Then said Jesus unto his disciples, If any man will come after me, let him deny himself, and take up his cross, and follow me. For whosoever will save his life shall lose it: and whosoever will lose his life for my sake shall find it*" (Matthew 16:24-25). To give up everything even our life needs a complete change to happen within us. "*And Satan answered the LORD, and said, Skin for skin, yea, all that a man hath will he give for his life*" (Job 2:4). That is why Jesus told Nicodemus, "*Verily, verily, I say unto thee, Except a man be born again, he cannot see the kingdom of God*" (John 3:3b). Even after received grace our tendencies are self preservation, but God by the working of the Holy Ghost gives knowledge in our heart that everything in this world is only temporary. His will works all things for the good of Christ's heavenly kingdom. "*And we know that all things work together for good to them that love God, to them who are the called according to his purpose*" (Romans 8:28). The result is contentment in the events that happen in our lives, even the station where God has put us. "*Not that I speak in respect of want: for I have learned, in whatsoever state I am, therewith to be content*" (Philippians 4:11). God who dwells in our hearts, brings us to look to the things for which He is preparing us, and gives comfort in life and death, "I do not belong to myself, but to my faithful Savior, Jesus Christ." And also, "*What? know ye not that your body is the temple of the Holy Ghost which is in you, which ye have of God, and ye are not your own? For ye are bought with a price: therefore glorify God in your body, and in your spirit, which are God's*" (1 Corinthians 6:19-20). God's will becomes our will more and more as we are conformed to the image of our Lord and Savior Jesus Christ.

> All the way my Savior leads me;
> what have I to ask beside?
> Can I doubt His tender mercy,
> Who thru life has been my guide?
> Heav'nly peace, divinest comfort.

Here by faith in Him to dwell!
For I know whate'er befall me,
Jesus doeth all things well.

All the way my Savior leads me;
Oh, the fullness of His love!
Perfect rest to me is promised
in my Father's house above:
When my spirit, cloth'd immortal,
wings its flight to realms of day,
This my song thru endless ages:
Jesus led me all the way.
Hymn by Fanny Crosby

69.
Bodily Necessities Provided

QUESTION: 125. WHICH IS THE fourth petition?

ANSWER: "GIVE US THIS DAY our daily bread"; that is, be pleased to provide us with all things necessary for the body, that we may thereby acknowledge Thee to be the only fountain of all good, and that neither our care nor industry, nor even Thy gifts, can profit us without Thy blessing; and therefore that we may withdraw our trust from all creatures, and place it alone in Thee.

God cares for His people, body and soul. He cares providentially for His whole creation. "*The eyes of all wait upon thee; and thou givest them their meat in due season. Thou openest thine hand, and satisfiest the desire of every living thing*" (Psalm 145:15-16). Nothing can survive without the blessing of God. "*God that made the world and all things therein, seeing that he is Lord of heaven and earth, dwelleth not in temples made with hands; Neither is worshipped with men's hands, as though he needed any thing, seeing he giveth to all life, and breath, and all things; And hath made of one blood all nations of men for to dwell on all the face of the earth, and hath determined the times before appointed, and the bounds of their habitation; That they should seek the Lord, if haply they might feel after him, and find him, though he be not far from every one of us: For in him we live, and move, and have our being"* (Acts 17:24-28a).

God hears the prayers of His people always, and they are the ones whose needs are supplied, benefiting those around them. *"That ye may be the children of your Father which is in heaven: for he maketh his sun to rise on the evil and on the good, and sendeth rain on the just and on the unjust"* (Matthew 5:45). O, the goodness of God toward us displays His love and the world seeing our gratitude for these blessings would cause them to seek Him too. *"Therefore thou art inexcusable, O man, whosoever thou art that judgest: for wherein thou judgest another, thou condemnest thyself; for thou that judgest doest the same things. Or despisest thou the riches of his goodness and forbearance and longsuffering; not knowing that the goodness of God leadeth thee to repentance"* (Romans 2:1 and 4). God gives strength in their journey through this wilderness to the blessedness of Jehovah's land, where want shall no more be heard or thought of.

> But let the righteous, blessed of yore,
> joy in their God as ne'er before,
> Faith's victory achieving,
> their joy shall then unbounded be
> Who see God's face eternally,
> their heart's desire receiving.

Exalt, exalt the Name of God;
sing ye His royal fame abroad
With fervent exultation;
cast up a highway smooth and wide
That through the deserts He may ride, J
ehovah, our salvation.
Psalter 420:2 for Psalm 68

70.
Our Debts Forgiven

QUESTION: 126. WHICH IS THE fifth petition?

ANSWER: "AND FORGIVE US OUR debts as we forgive our debtors"; that is, be pleased for the sake of Christ's blood, not to impute to us poor sinners, our transgressions, nor that depravity, which always cleaves to us; even as we feel this evidence of Thy grace in us, that is our firm resolution from the heart to forgive our neighbor.

One of the hardest things we are required to do is to forgive those who hurt us. We will say, "I forgive you", but still harbor doubts in our heart thinking, "I cannot forget." This reveals the pride in our hearts. Pride is the sin which will drag us down unless Jesus, as He said to Peter, "*Simon, Simon, behold, Satan hath desired to have you, that he may sift you as wheat: But I have prayed for thee, that thy faith fail not: and when thou art converted, strengthen thy brethren*" (Luke 22"31-32). Pride comes in many different forms, but all end up the same. It is all about

ME! Christ warned the people, "*But if ye do not forgive, neither will your Father which is in heaven forgive your trespasses*" (Mark 11:26). Unforgiven sins between people separate. We just do not feel comfortable in their presence and avoid them. It is the same in spiritual life. Adam when He had disobeyed and heard God walking in the cool of the day, hid himself (Read Genesis 3.) God comes and calls us, and we come trembling expecting the worst, but hear from Him, "I will forgive their iniquity, and I will remember their sin no more" Jeremiah 31:34b). If the holy God can forgive and forget our sin, our prayer should be, "Lord, help me to forgive those who angered me, as Thou hast forgiven me." The faithful and true God in Jesus Christ has said, "*Whatsoever ye shall ask the Father in my name, he will give it you. Hitherto have ye asked nothing in my name: ask, and ye shall receive, that your joy may be full*" (John 16:24b-25). This is the only comfort in life and in death that I do not belong to myself, but to my faithful Savior, Jesus Christ as the catechism begins. We cannot do with less, but more is not needed.

May the grace of Christ, the Savior,
And the Father's boundless love,
With the Holy Spirit's favor
Rest upon us from above.

Thus may we abide in union,
With each other, and the Lord,
And possess in sweet communion,
Joys which earth cannot afford.
Doxology

71.
God Our only Deliverer

QUESTION: 127. WHICH IS THE sixth petition?

ANSWER: "AND LEAD US NOT into temptation, but deliver us from evil"; that is; since we are so weak in ourselves, that we cannot stand a moment; and besides this, since our mortal enemies the devil, the world, and our own flesh, cease not to assault us, do Thou therefore preserve and strengthen us by the power of Thy Holy Spirit, that we may not be overcome in this spiritual warfare, but constantly and strenuously may resist our foes, till at last we obtain complete victory.

There are so many things which draw us away from God. The devil fills our mind with all kinds of sins. The world is used by Satan to take our eye and heart off of eternal things. Our ears, eyes, feet, hands, and tongue, yes, our hearts are things which cause much sorrow and without the Holy Spirit we would despair and eventually destroy ourselves. *"All we like sheep have gone astray; we have turned every one to his own way; and the*

LORD *hath laid on him the iniquity of us all*" (Isaiah 53:6). Jesus taught His disciples how to pray. He knew their proneness to fall into temptations even though they loved their Shepherd. As the Psalmist they cry, "*I have gone astray like a lost sheep; seek thy servant; for I do not forget thy commandments*" Psalm 119:176). Sheep must be sought after. They cannot find their way back to the flock alone. Jesus, the Son of God, came to do that, and today sends His servants with His Word, "*For the Son of man is come to seek and to save that which was lost*" (Luke 19:10). The Son of man did not only come to seek, but save lost, hell-worthy sheep by cleansing them from all their sins in that "fountain opened for sin and uncleanness," as we read in Zechariah 13:1. We are taught this by the Shepherd, Jesus Christ through the working of the Holy Spirit. This is comfort indeed. Yes, the only comfort in life and in death.

> Amazing Grace! How sweet the sound,
> that saved a wretch like me!
> I once was lost but now am found,
> was blind by now I see.

> 'Twas grace that taught my heart to fear,
> and grace my fears relieved;
> How precious did that grace appear
> the hour I first believed.

> The Lord has promised good to me,
> His word my hope secures;
> He will my shield and portion be
> as long as life endures.

Thru many dangers, toils, and snares,
I have already come;
'Tis grace hath brought me safe thus far,
and grace will lead me home.

When we've been there ten thousand years,
bright shining as the sun,
We've no less days to sing God's praise
than when we'd first begun.
Hymn by John Newton

72.
Doxology

QUESTION: 128. How dost thou conclude thy prayer?

ANSWER: "For Thine is the kingdom, and the power, and the glory, for ever"; that is, all these we ask of thee, because Thou; being our King and Almighty, art willing and able to give us all good; and all this we pray for, that thereby not we but thy holy Name, may be glorified for ever.

QUESTION: 129. What doth the word "Amen" signify?

ANSWER: "Amen" signifies, it shall truly and certainly be: for my prayer is more assuredly heard of God, than I feel in my heart that I desire these things of Him.

In our travel through the Catechism the theme and question asked becomes more and more precious. Although we have failed so many times God has never failed, yea, He has fulfilled His promise to never forsake the works of His hand! Job saw it and in all his trouble cried out, *"For I know that my redeemer liveth, and that he shall stand at the latter day upon the earth: And though after my skin worms destroy this body, yet in my flesh shall I see God: Whom I shall see for myself, and mine eyes shall behold, and not another*" (Job 19:25-27a). His people are safe in Him forever as Jesus said, "*In the world ye shall have tribulation: but be of good cheer; I have overcome the world*" (John 16:33b). May our eyes be lifted up to the throne of grace where He sits at the right hand of power interceding for His people every moment! "Now unto God and our Father be glory for ever and ever. Amen" (Philippians 4:20).

Our song forever shall record the tender mercies of our God! "*Comfort ye, comfort ye my people, saith your God. Speak ye comfortably to Jerusalem, and cry unto her, that her warfare is accomplished, that her iniquity is pardoned: for she hath received of the Lord's hand double for all her sins*" (Isaiah 40:1-2). He is the Great Amen, all glory, might, and power end in Him alone. "*After this I beheld, and, lo, a great multitude, which no man could number, of all nations, and kindreds, and people, and tongues, stood before the throne, and before the Lamb, clothed with white robes, and palms in their hands; And cried with a loud voice, saying, Salvation to our God which sitteth upon the throne, and unto the Lamb. And all the angels stood round about the throne, and about the elders and the four beasts, and fell before the throne on their faces, and worshipped God, Saying, Amen: Blessing, and glory, and wisdom, and thanksgiving, and honour, and power, and might, be unto our God for ever and ever. Amen*" (Revelation 7:9-12).

Come ye that fear Jehovah,
ye saints your voices raise;
Come stand in awe before Him,
and sing His glorious praise,
Ye lowly and afflicted
who on His word rely,
Your heart shall live forever,
the Lord will satisfy.

Both high and low shall worship,
both strong and weak shall bend,
A faithful church shall serve Him
till generations end,
His praise shall be recounted
to nations yet to be,
The triumphs of His justice
a new born world shall see.
Psalter 50:1 and 3

Other titles available from Reformation Heritage Books

(616) 977-0889 or www.heritagebooks.org:

A series of "Meditations of the heart"
12 booklets of 31-35 meditations each
1. A Watered Garden
2. Hidden Manna
3. Eternal Light
4. Harvest Gleaning
5. Haven of Rest
6. Looking for Jesus
7. The Divine Physician
8. Songs of Deliverance
9. Kernels of Truth
10. Feed My Sheep
11. Alive in Christ
12. Zion in View

Cornelius VanKempen
Blog: http://casey4949.wordpress.com
Casevankempen4949@gmail.com or casey4949@comcast.net

Made in the USA
Middletown, DE
22 May 2017